The Vanishing Virtue

The Vanishing Virtue

Empowering Your Journey to Unshakable Belief

By

Jaren L Davis

Independently published

Printed in the United States of America

ISBN: 9781088245040

Dedication

To my loved ones, the divine guides in my life, and the countless individuals who unknowingly played a part in shaping my journey,

This book, born from a profound concern for our world's direction and a longing for something greater than ourselves, is a testament to the power of faith. It is a culmination of two years of heartfelt introspection and an unwavering belief that there is hope amidst uncertainty.

To my dear parents and grandparents, whose unwavering support and unconditional love have been a source of strength, I am forever grateful. Your wisdom and nurturing hearts have shaped me into the person I am today.

To my beloved wife, Kim, and our cherished children—Jake, Katie, Sallie, and Lindie—your unwavering belief in me and your patience has been a constant source of inspiration. You are the embodiment of love and faith in my life.

I extend my gratitude to the many friends, acquaintances, and strangers turned kindred spirits who unknowingly guided me through their words of advice and counsel. Through podcasts, talks, writings, interviews, and videos, you touched my soul and instilled a renewed sense of purpose. Your collective influence led me to discover the comfort and solace of expressing my thoughts from the depths of my heart.

This dedication is not only an expression of appreciation but a fervent hope that my humble words may touch the life of even one person, igniting a spark of faith and guiding them toward a future filled with possibility.

May the echoes of gratitude and hope contained within these pages resonate with someone, somewhere, sometime, and in some way, bringing light to their journey and nourishing their spirit.

With heartfelt gratitude,

Jaren Lee Davis

Praise for "The Vanishing Virtue" by Jaren Davis

With 'Vanishing Virtue,' I aimed to touch the hearts and provoke the thoughts of readers from all walks of life. I am grateful for the feedback I've received, a few of which are shared below…

Darrell Lee Scharman

'The Vanishing Virtue' is a riveting read that immediately drew me in with its expertly woven narrative. This beautifully crafted book, rich with wisdom on every page, offered a profound, transformative experience, putting it on par with works by esteemed authors like Dr. Wayne Dyer.

Heather Osmond

Jaren, with 'The Vanishing Virtue', architects a riveting journey in faith's realm, an exploration that's a rare find. Trust me when I say this: the book is to be treasured, experienced, and revisited time and again.

Sunny Banks

In "The Vanishing Virtue", Jaren seamlessly combines historical information, spiritual insight, and personal stories. His thoughtful prose invites readers to reflect on faith, virtue, and love, providing a pathway for personal transformation. This blend of enjoyment and inspiration makes Jaren's book a uniquely enriching read, spotlighting his genuine concern for each reader's journey.

Dan Smith

The book, "Vanishing Virtue" by Jaren Davis is one of the greats! It pulls together the wisdom literature of the years in a way that you choose to keep turning the pages! The book is engaging as it hits on the core principles of faith and how it can change our lives for the better. Jaren shares powerful quotes, stories and examples that make this a handbook for both our personal and professional lives.

Anne Oborn

Jaren's book, 'The Vanishing Virtue', offers a uniquely insightful exploration of faith, skillfully drawing from diverse cultural and personal experiences. With its emotionally impactful narrative, the book beautifully exemplifies the essence of love and mercy, evoking a profound response that leaves the reader deeply moved and eager to engage further in this enlightening journey.

Dan Hogan

Much of what we get out of life--and put into it--relates to the people we encounter and the models we use to interpret these encounters. Typical of Jaren Davis's approach to life, he invites us here to think broadly and live genuinely with life models and real people that bring peace and hope to our sometimes disheveled lives.

Jeff Adams

A well written, thought-provoking book, exploring our own paths to Faith. It teaches us that no matter how things around us may appear, the uniqueness of our experiences can inspire us to regain and build our faith. A great read regardless of where you find yourself on the spectrum of faith.

Sharrin Miller

"Vanishing Virtue" by Jaren Davis is a tour de force that left me deeply moved and with an almost depleted highlighter. His eloquent exploration of faith has helped me better understand the void many of us experience in our lives. His words are a call to introspection and reevaluation, challenging us to stay true to our beliefs against all odds. As a woman of strong faith, I resonate with Davis' perspectives and am empowered by his courage to stand firm in the face of criticism. This enlightening work is a treasure I intend to share widely, urging everyone I meet to dive into its wisdom-filled pages. Davis' valuable message of hope is a testament to his commitment to nurturing spiritual growth. I am profoundly grateful to him for sharing his insights, providing a guide to a more fulfilling life.

Ty Vranes

Jaren Davis's "Vanishing Virtue" is a masterstroke in understanding faith and its essential role in unlocking our true potential. As a man of deep religious conviction, I've devoted my life to service and personal growth, cherishing the wisdom I uncover. Davis's thought-provoking narratives and powerful insights gave me new perspectives, helping me recalibrate my compass towards my true north. It's a book that doesn't just grace your shelves, but makes a home in your heart, urging you to delve deeper into the labyrinth of your soul. My sincerest hope is that "Vanishing Virtue" finds its way into the hands of many, igniting in them a desire for self-discovery and understanding. Davis's exemplary portrayal of faith is a testament to his commitment towards fostering spiritual growth and it's an honor to witness and learn from his journey.

Kim Horn

Jaren Davis's "Vanishing Virtue" stands out as an insightful exploration of the challenging issues we face today, addressing them with a rare blend of grace and pragmatism. As a professional woman who balances a successful career with raising a family, my moments of leisure are few, yet each opportunity I find to delve into Davis's work is an enriching experience.

Davis's profound faith in humanity resonates with my own beliefs, his wisdom echoing the necessity for our generation to lead by example. His articulation of life's truths, gleaned from his own experiences, serves as a beacon for a better society. This book is a testament to the impact that a well-lived life of principle and virtue can make.

"Vanishing Virtue" is more than a book, it's a call to action, inspiring us to elevate ourselves and our communities. To Jaren Davis, my deepest appreciation for sharing your insights, for they have left an indelible imprint on my journey towards personal and societal improvement.

Carol Wallace

Life doesn't present many things capable of stealing me away from the exquisite pleasure of a chilled Diet Coke soothing my throat while basking in the sun on a picturesque beach. However, The Vanishing Virtue by Jaren Davis has done just that. The question is: why? The answer may not be entirely clear, but I surmise it's rooted in the glimmer of hope the book provides - the promise that our future can swerve from its current trajectory and navigate towards an era where growth and prosperity are possible for all.

Davis's work insists that we revitalize our senses to truly grasp the magnitude of our existence. It implores us to reflect upon our values and virtues, ones that seem to be vanishing in today's world. These insightful observations prompted me to revisit The Vanishing Virtue for a second reading. As if a breath of fresh air in our often chaotic world, this book has not just captured my attention but also stirred an optimistic anticipation for what lies ahead.

Josh Ward

As a physician who frequently grapples with life-threatening situations, I find Jaren Davis's "Vanishing Virtue" to be a much-needed compass in understanding the interplay between faith and my medical practice. This enlightening read beautifully bridges the gap between spiritual insight and the pragmatic realities of life, drawing parallels with the life-affirming triumphs and trials I witness daily.

Davis's unwavering belief in a divine plan resonates with my own conviction of a Creator, offering reassurance in the face of daily challenges. For anyone seeking to unravel the mystery of our existence, "Vanishing Virtue" serves as an illuminating guide, reinforcing the belief in a purpose-driven life.

Bill Armstrong

In "The Vanishing Virtue", Jaren Davis eloquently brings to light the core issues of our time. His keen insights into our societal trajectory are not just sobering, but inspiring. His exploration of faith as our potential saving grace resonates deeply, particularly with contemplative minds such as mine. With incisive clarity and candor, Davis gives the wake-up call that many in our government and society at large desperately need. His book is not only a critique but also a beacon of hope, demonstrating a path forward through faith. We owe a debt of gratitude to Davis for confronting these societal issues head-on and striving to make a positive difference. His work is a call to action that will stir many to self-reflection and possibly, to transformative action.

Paul Jones

What Jaren Davis has done with The Vanishing Virtue is reignite a once respected, but now widely ignored literary genre called "mirrors for princes." The Prince, by Machiavelli, is a prominent example, as is the City of God by Augustine, George Washington tried his hand at the genre with his 110 personal maxims he called, The Rules of Civility and Decent Behavior.

In the genre, which date back to the Sumerians and Egyptians, experienced and accomplished people pass on to young princes what they've learned about how best to navigate an ever-shifting world, all while keeping one's humanity.

The "mirrors for princes" genre is commonly political. But Davis's Vanishing Virtue carves out a different topic to reflect on: Faith. In doing so, Davis is certainly spiritual, even religious from time to time, but not preachy or didactic.

Vanishing Virtue is a book of Davis's accumulated wisdom on the necessity of keeping faith with God and self and mankind in our increasingly faithless times. It reads well. There's depth and nuance in every page and wisdom in every chapter.

Best of all, you don't have to be a young royal to benefit from reading it!

The heartening response to 'Vanishing Virtue' speaks volumes about its transformative impact on readers' lives. What will your journey with 'Vanishing Virtue' inspire in you? Read on, and join us in the exploration of faith, personal growth, and the essence of humanity.

'Vanishing Virtue' by Jaren Davis is available now in bookstores and through popular online retailers. Stay connected with Jaren through his website jarenldavis.com and social media platforms for updates about upcoming events, talks, and signings. Thank you for considering this enriching journey into faith, virtue, and personal growth.

TABLE OF CONTENTS

PROLOGUE

In the gentle, quiet moments before dawn, as the stars twinkle their last for the night and the first threads of sunlight start to sew a new day into the fabric of time, we find ourselves in a space of profound peace. In these moments of solitude, we often seek solace, solace in something far greater than ourselves, a power that transcends our earthly existence. This is the journey into faith.

From time immemorial, faith has been a cornerstone of human existence. A beacon of hope in the darkness, a compass in the wilderness of uncertainty, a foundation upon which societies have been built and thrived. Not merely a belief in a higher power, faith extends to the relationships we forge, the people we encounter, and the society we inhabit. It is the invisible thread that weaves through the rich panorama of our lives, often unrecognized but always present.

Imagine a world without faith. It would be akin to a ship adrift in a turbulent sea without a compass. Faith, in its many forms, gives us a reason to trust, to hope, and to believe in the potential for better days. We place our faith in our families, our friends, our leaders, and the institutions that govern our lives. This faith, even if tested or shaken, reinforces the social fabric that binds us together. It is the glue that holds the jigsaw puzzle of society intact.

The path to faith, however, is not a smooth one. It's a journey marked by questions, doubts, and, sometimes, painful lessons. It's a journey that requires courage and resilience. Yet, those who embark on this journey know that every step, every stumble, and every leap of faith is a step closer to understanding and wisdom. This book is a tribute to those brave souls, a hand of friendship extended to those who are on the path of building their faith.

In the pages that follow, we delve into the labyrinth of faith, exploring its many dimensions, its trials and triumphs, its complexities and simplicities. Whether you are a seasoned traveler in this journey or just taking your first tentative steps, this book is for you. It is an invitation to open your mind, to question, to reflect, and to discover the profound impact of faith on our lives.

As we delve into this exploration of faith, let's remember that faith does not demand perfection. It understands our human frailties, our doubts, and our mistakes. It meets us where we are and leads us to where we need to be. It whispers in our ear that it's okay to stumble as long as we pick ourselves up, dust ourselves off, and continue our journey.

In essence, this book is an exploration, a guide, and a companion on your journey of faith. It is a testament to the human spirit and its endless quest for understanding. It's a celebration of faith in all its forms and its profound role in shaping our lives and our world.

Faith has been and always will be a cornerstone of human existence. Its power is immeasurable, its impact profound. It is the foundation upon which we build our lives and our societies. So, as the new day dawns and the stars give way to the rising sun, let's embark on this journey of discovery, of understanding, of faith. Let's begin!

CHAPTER ONE

Faiths Role in Society

In the heart of Rome, the echoes of a once vibrant civilization bounced off the marble columns and empty courtyards. It was the time when the Roman Empire, once the cradle of civilization, stood on the precipice of decline. Their arenas, once filled with valorous gladiators and a captivated public, had turned into sites of cruel decadence. The senators, who once held the wisdom of governance, succumbed to internal power struggles, corruption, and excesses. The common folk, distracted by bread and circuses, lost sight of their collective purpose. The virtues that had once underpinned their society – courage, wisdom, justice, and discipline – were eroded by the sands of complacency.

Throughout history, such scenarios have been far too common. Civilizations have risen and fallen in seemingly endless cycles. Often, the downfall of these great societies, like the Roman Empire, came as people lost sight of their purpose. Prosperity, which should have been a boon, bred a dangerous sense of pride and boredom. As wealth accumulated, attitudes shifted inward toward the pursuit of temporary pleasures. The citizens, intoxicated by the illusion of unending prosperity, became blind to the cracks forming at the foundation of their society.

When we observe this pattern, we realize that the first steps toward the decline of goodness among citizens occur when individual fortune causes a loss of that inner compass designed to guide us through life.

Reflect on our modern times. A study conducted by the Pew Research Center in 2019 showed that the percentage of adults identifying as religiously unaffiliated was on the rise - from 17% in 2009 to 26% in 2019 in the United States. This group, also known as 'nones,' consists of people who describe their religious identity as atheist, agnostic or 'nothing in particular.' The rise in religiously unaffiliated individuals corresponds to the decline of Christians and other religious communities.

In addition to these overarching trends, personal worship and the pursuit of meaning are also diminishing. We see this in our digital age, where people spend hours each day on social media, engaging in fleeting interactions and consuming ephemeral content, while rarely taking the time for introspection or to ponder life's deeper purpose.

Observe also the disheartening news headlines that paint a picture of moral decay - stories of corporate corruption, political scandal, and community disarray. These stories serve as the pulse of a society where the search for personal significance and greater purpose seems to be waning. Our society, much like the ancient Romans, risks losing its moral compass in the face of prosperity and distraction.

Evidence of this falling away from our inner light is apparent in the world today, and manifests in various forms. One such instance is the declining faith in our institutions. This can be seen in our rapidly changing world where trust in government, media, and even healthcare systems has eroded. Misinformation spreads, conspiracy theories thrive, and skepticism has become a default response. This erosion of trust suggests a collective dimming of our inner light as we grow disillusioned with the structures meant to uphold society.

Another indication is the societal division over nationalism, populism, and policy. Across the globe, we see an increasing fragmentation along ideological lines. The unity that once characterized neighborhoods, communities, and even countries appears to be dissolving, replaced by factionalism and a stubborn unwillingness to engage in constructive dialogue. The rise of social media echo chambers and the polarization of political views signal a faltering commitment to principles of mutual respect and understanding.

The war in Europe and escalating global conflicts are further signs of this loss. These conflicts reflect our collective failure to resolve differences peacefully, indicating a retreat from the sacred path that calls us to strive for harmony and reconciliation.

On top of these global issues, we also grapple with growing socio-economic disparity. The gap between the rich and the poor continues to widen, creating an environment of resentment and disillusionment. While prosperity abounds for a few, many are left grappling with poverty, insecurity, and a sense of injustice.

Moreover, the lingering conditions from the pandemic have cast long shadows over our world. The healthcare crisis, job loss, prolonged isolation, and mental health struggles have led many to question their purpose, triggering a personal crisis of faith and identity.

More personal instances may include loss of identity, feelings of self-worth, and confusion as to one's purpose. As our light dims, we lean toward makeshift relief from a soul yearning to break free from these bonds. In a world that increasingly values external achievements and accolades, it's easy for individuals to feel lost and disconnected from their inner selves.

The loss of our inner moral compass is a pervasive issue affecting both our collective societies and individual lives. As we navigate these troubled times, the need to reconnect with our core values and inner light becomes ever more critical.

History has shown that society flourishes when its citizens actively engage in principles discovered by those who have learned to follow their guiding star. This light is universal, boundless, and naturally infuses a soul with goodness. It directs us outward, finding strength in the lasting happiness that comes from working together.

Evidence of this heavenly map, the inner compass that directs us toward wisdom and moral living, can be found in both broad and specific instances. Regardless of cultural, religious, or ideological differences, the fundamental essence of this light remains the same.

At the core of Eastern and Western thought are similarities, defined by different words, but grounded on the same bedrock of human characteristics. Take, for instance, the concepts of compassion, honesty, and resilience. These principles hold true whether you lean toward Islam, Buddhism, Chinese wisdom, Christianity, or Judaism.

Think about the story of Abdul Sattar Edhi, a philanthropist from Pakistan. He lived his life serving others, setting up the largest volunteer ambulance network in Pakistan. His faith in Islam and its principles of charity and selflessness guided him. Despite facing numerous challenges, he held fast to his inner light, showing us the transformative power of leading a purpose-driven life.

In the West, we have examples such as Martin Luther King Jr., a beacon of light during the American civil rights movement. Guided by his Christian faith and commitment to justice, he strove tirelessly to challenge segregation and champion equal rights. His ability to stir the conscience of a nation illustrates the impact one individual, firmly grounded in their inner light, can make.

In the realm of Buddhism, we see individuals like Thich Nhat Hanh, a renowned monk who devoted his life to the promotion of mindfulness and peace. Despite experiencing the horrors of the Vietnam War, he held steadfastly to his beliefs, demonstrating the resilience and inner strength that comes from adhering to one's inner light.

Turning toward societies, we see nations such as Bhutan that have chosen to define success not solely by material wealth, but by Gross National Happiness, a metric that evaluates spiritual, physical, social, and environmental health of its citizens. This demonstrates a collective pursuit of a higher purpose and illustrates the benefits that can arise when a society commits to following its inner light.

In each of these instances, both individuals and societies have demonstrated the power and impact of adhering to their guiding principles and inner light, fostering an environment of resilience, progress, and harmony.

On a smaller scale, the inner light continues to guide us, even when we choose to find our answers outside traditional religious or philosophical systems. Even if you are agnostic or inclined to seek wisdom in the works of great artists, writers, and thinkers, their teachings illuminate the same fundamental truths.

Assess the writings of William Shakespeare, whose profound insights into human nature remain relevant to this day. His characters, flawed yet aspirational, seek redemption, justice, and love, reflecting our collective striving toward goodness. His works, such as "King Lear" or "Hamlet," present dilemmas of moral choices and the pursuit of purpose, reminding us of our inherent inner light that guides us toward ethical living.

Michelangelo, the renowned Italian artist, instilled his artworks with deep spiritual and humanistic themes. His sculpture 'David' or his painting on the ceiling of the Sistine Chapel are not just displays of exceptional artistic skill, but are also rich in philosophical and moral symbolism. They reflect a man who was led by his inner light to create works that continue to inspire and challenge us on our moral and spiritual journeys.

Literary figures like Leo Tolstoy and Charles Dickens, despite their different cultural contexts, wrote stories that delve into the human condition, exploring themes of morality, justice, and redemption. Tolstoy, with his masterpiece "War and Peace," and Dickens with works such as "A Tale of Two Cities" and "Great Expectations," demonstrated the universal principles of good and evil, compassion, and the pursuit of justice, resonating with our inner light.

Historical figures like Confucius, Joan of Arc, or Francis of Assisi, each in their unique way, lived their lives guided by their inner light. Confucius shaped an entire culture with his teachings on ethics and personal virtue. Joan of Arc, motivated by her religious beliefs and a vision of justice and freedom, led armies to victory. Francis of Assisi abandoned worldly riches to live a life of poverty and service, his actions mirroring his deep commitment to peace and love.

As Mother Teresa once said, "There is a light in this world, a healing spirit more powerful than any darkness we may encounter. We sometimes lose sight of this force when there is suffering, too much pain. Then suddenly, the spirit will emerge through the lives of ordinary people who hear a call and answer in extraordinary ways." These individuals, each in their unique way, demonstrate that every single person is guided by an inner light originating from the same source. Their lives and works continue to inspire and remind us of the profound wisdom and compassion we are capable of when we adhere to our inner light.

To better understand these core principles, let's revisit the parable of the Good Samaritan from the Bible. A man, presumably of Jewish faith, is assaulted by robbers and left to die on a lonely road. Two figures from his own community, a priest and a Levite, pass him by, ignoring his desperate situation. Yet, it's a Samaritan, regarded as a societal outsider, who stops to help. He tends to the man's wounds, takes him to an inn, and provides for his care. This Samaritan, guided by his inner light of compassion and charity, acts as a true neighbor. His action underscores the universal nature of our inner light, transcending societal divisions and religious boundaries.

For instance, a core principle of Confucianism is benevolence, harmony, and courtesy. Buddhism emphasizes compassion and selflessness. Christianity, as taught by Paul the Apostle, centers on faith, hope, and charity. The commonality of these primary drivers is benevolence, compassion, and charity.

Can we say there is any difference between these three words? No, they are the same, and the inner light at the core of these inspired leaders is the same, regardless of the term used. It is proof that the inspired teachings come from the same source, a Being, no matter our descriptor, who is our Creator. Not only our Maker but also the Designer of the world in which we live and the Author of a plan designed for our good.

A Creator whose purpose is to help us find that proverbial drop of honey on a blade of grass, to realize that our position between a rock and a hard place is temporary and ultimately for our good. That in this life, we can find deep inner joy, that we are part of an eternal plan designed for our happiness, and that this happiness will be unending.

If divinity has guided humanity to use these descriptors across ages and continents, we should pause to weigh what value they may bring to our lives. The similarities should resonate with an open heart and mind, finding a home where they can flourish. These similarities unite us, both in larger groups and as individuals, seeking to bring about good. They may guide us down different paths, yet all lead to the same destination: a place where the spark of our inner light ignites a flame that leads us to a fulfilling life designed for our growth, bringing us joy and preparing us for eternity. "Out beyond ideas of wrongdoing and rightdoing, there is a field. I'll meet you there. When the soul lies down in that grass, the world is too full to talk about." - Rumi.

When we open ourselves to the teachings of others, we expand our learning beyond what is typically found when we close ourselves off to outside perspectives. If we concentrate on these core principles, we will find a foundation that is consistent with a unifying spirit, tethering us to a Creator who yearns for our wellbeing.

However, the complexity of our present-day arises when differences are promoted. These ideas are propagated by closed minds, driven to add concepts that meet personal objectives. For these individuals, being right has become more important than focusing on goodness. This can be observed in many organized groups, including religions, where layers are added to the core teachings, obscuring what truly matters.

When we focus with our hearts, our spiritual anchor celebrates our differences, recognizing the collective good that can be achieved as we look outward. We must focus on the core elements taught to us as we begin to discern our purpose. Celebrating these common cores allows us to find peace and build healthy societies on advancements.

Jesus of Nazareth taught us to love our neighbor and our enemy, to pray for those who cause us harm. The wisdom of these words lies in focusing on the similarities found in the core principles. With an eye directed in this way, we can resolve differences through understanding.

Try to understand others' perspectives, particularly those who may hold differing viewpoints from your own. Remember that each person you encounter is undergoing their unique journey and challenges.

Little things can trigger big things when no one is paying attention to their light of wisdom. Remember the 1969 Woodstock disaster, where factors contributed to destruction and chaos. Attendees, under the influence of a collective negative energy, may have acted out of character, abandoning all sense of kindness, understanding, and nobility. Yet, in each excuse, we can see someone straying from their core. Amid such circumstances, it's understandable why one woman reportedly commented that she would never trust a man again.

Yet, these same people could have acted differently if they had been tethered to something meaningful, or if natural leaders had countered escalating negative emotions with the calmness found in following their inner light. If someone had slowed the momentum rather than igniting a flame, we would be reading a different history of that event. This holds true for most situations where offense, misunderstanding, or a focus on differences ruled the day.

Imagine two groups of people in the afterlife. One group is told by the Creator, "Your forms of worship were wrong, but you were benevolent, compassionate, and charitable." I believe He would welcome this group, knowing He could correct any misguided doctrine should it be necessary.

To the other group, He might say, "You got the doctrine correct, your creeds were on point, yet your self-righteousness and intolerance left much to be desired." This group might find it more challenging to become who they are meant to be.

Victor Hugo's 'Les Misérables' provides a compelling case for the transformative power of benevolence and compassion. Jean Valjean, hardened by years in prison, begins as a character defined by bitterness and mistrust, a man lost in the darkness of his circumstances and choices. The turning point comes with his encounter with Bishop Myriel, a man who is a beacon of goodness, kindness, and understanding.

The Bishop's actions toward Valjean go beyond conventional morality. He not only forgives Valjean for his betrayal but also empowers him to change the course of his life. By claiming that the stolen silverware was a gift, the bishop protects Valjean from further punishment. He then privately gives Valjean two silver candlesticks, not only offering material aid but also imbuing this gift with a moral obligation – to use this opportunity to become an honest man.

This pivotal moment sets Valjean on a transformative journey toward redemption. The bishop's compassion becomes the catalyst that rekindles Valjean's inner light, the innate goodness that had been stifled by years of hardship and injustice. His life transforms drastically, from a man full of resentment to a compassionate benefactor who positively impacts the lives of numerous characters, like the desperate Fantine and her daughter Cosette.

Moreover, the ripple effect of the bishop's kindness resonates throughout the narrative, illustrating the broader implications of such acts of benevolence. Every instance of kindness, understanding, and generosity that Valjean extends to others can be traced back to that pivotal encounter with Bishop Myriel. It's a powerful testament to how our actions, guided by our inner light, can illuminate the path for others, triggering a chain reaction of goodness.

The story of Jean Valjean is a call to each of us to embrace and express our inner light, as Bishop Myriel did. It invites us to think about how our acts of compassion can not only transform individual lives but also send ripples of positive change throughout our communities. Indeed, when we choose to act with kindness and understanding, we are acknowledging the inner light in ourselves and others, contributing to a world defined more by empathy and unity, rather than division and resentment.

Be intentional; this could be as simple as holding the door open for someone, offering a smile to a stranger, or calling a friend who might be having a tough day. Small acts of kindness can have a profound impact on both the giver and the receiver.

I'm certain that, despite our uniqueness, our heart wants us to embody those core principles that enable everyone, regardless of the path chosen, to do good for all humanity. "The best way to find yourself is to lose yourself in the service of others." - Mahatma Gandhi.

Our task is to navigate our life experiences maintaining a connection to what we have found to be true. Your stronghold should be tied to benevolence, compassion, and charity. From the security of this foundation, you can freely seek additional truth that enables you to become all you are meant to be—without limitation.

If you ever question your faith, acknowledging the presence of doubt doesn't mean you are sacrificing the truths you have learned. We learn by questioning and then holding onto those foundational truths that lie in a humble heart. When we accept uncertainties that we can't dismiss given our human limitations, we grow. Your search should be conducted not to disprove, but to learn. Often, the answers we seek aren't necessary for our progression at the moment, so they can wait. "The measure of intelligence is the ability to change." - Albert Einstein.

Regularly take time to reflect on your actions, attitudes, and choices. Ask yourself, "Am I being as compassionate as I can be? Am I practicing charity and benevolence in my daily interactions?

You are on the right path when your answers bring about goodness. As you test these answers, evaluate whether they persuade you to do good. There is much in our world to help us, provided by others who have followed their light. We will explore these later in the book, including personal stories and other engagements, but our discussion will focus on human achievement.

Seek with a sincere heart, knowing that the gentle whispers you hear will be the beginning of a faith that can withstand any storm. Even if it means believing in another until that still small voice begins to speak to your heart.

CHAPTER TWO

The Dawn of Faith: Understanding the Basics

Within the quietest corners of our heart resides a spark, a delicate flicker, a subtle whisper of faith. Unassuming and yet potent, this spark carries the remarkable potential to grow and flourish, much like a tiny seed that, when planted in fertile soil, evolves into a robust tree providing shelter, nourishment, and supporting abundant life. The journey of faith, in its most beautiful simplicity, commences with such a seed planted in the fertile grounds of our receptive spirit.

Faith is a universal language; it defies borders, transcends diverse cultures, and creates an invisible, yet tangible bond that connects hearts worldwide. Regardless of our unique beliefs, varied backgrounds, or vast range of experiences, each one of us holds within us this spark of faith. It fuels hope in the face of despair, trust in the midst of doubts, and peace within chaos.

To delve deeper into the essence of faith, we must ask, what truly is faith? At its core, faith is belief - a belief in the unseen, the unproven, the unfathomable. It's a profound conviction that there's an omnipotent entity guiding our lives, a design to our existence, and more to life than what simply meets the eye. However, faith transcends mere belief; it is about trust. It's about entrusting our lives, our destinies, our futures to this higher power, in the steadfast assurance that even when life's tempests batter us, we stand firmly rooted.

Venturing into this exploration of faith, let us approach with an open heart and an open mind. This is not a journey designed for the faint-hearted but a path that calls for courage to question, to seek, to step into the realm of the unknown. Yet, this courage is not beyond our reach; it resides within each one of us, silently waiting to be invoked.

The voyage to faith doesn't follow a straight, predictable line. Instead, it meanders like a riveting road full of twists and turns, marked by towering mountains and deep valleys, moments of sunshine and inevitable storms. There will be times when faith feels as tangible as the firm ground beneath our feet. And there will be instances when faith seems as elusive as a mirage shimmering in a scorching desert. Yet, it is within these intervals of doubt and confusion that our faith undergoes refinement, becoming deeper, stronger, and more resilient. It is within the crucible of questioning that our comprehension of faith broadens and matures.

The exploration of faith is not a solitary endeavor. We walk alongside the footprints of countless individuals throughout history who have embarked on this journey before us, each leaving behind a trail of wisdom for us to follow and a legacy of faith for us to learn from. Their stories, experiences, trials, and triumphs will provide a roadmap as we navigate this profound journey.

As we delve deeper, it is important to remember that faith is an incredibly personal and unique experience. Your path and understanding of faith may look nothing like mine, and that's perfectly okay. Faith isn't about conforming to the norm; it's about authenticity, about finding your individual path, your truth, your unique understanding.

Let us also acknowledge that faith is not a static concept; it is dynamic and evolutionary. It matures and evolves as we do, growing in tandem with our personal and spiritual development. It is not merely a destination to be reached, but a fascinating journey to be experienced. So, as we embark on this exploration of faith, let's do so with unbridled curiosity, heartfelt compassion, and a sense of exhilarating adventure.

Welcome, then, to the dawn of faith. At the very start of this journey, we stand on the threshold of an odyssey that promises to be transformative, enlightening, and profoundly impactful. Regardless of whether you are a seasoned traveler in the realm of faith or a novice, whether you are brimming with certainty or grappling with doubts, know that you are welcome here. This journey is universal, embracing everyone, and it begins with a single, courageous step - a step of faith.

— Let the transformative journey begin —

Our exploration of faith aims to illuminate the heart and enlighten the mind, providing a newfound depth and understanding that resonates with every soul willing to embark on this journey. By shedding light on this complex yet beautiful concept, we hope to spark an awakening, a dawn of faith that is unique to each person but universally beckons to all who are willing to listen and explore.

My hope in offering this text is to provide a well of wisdom, insight, and understanding about faith, equipping us with the tools to navigate life's uncertainties and challenges. The wisdom shared here is designed to captivate, inspire, and provide a peaceful reassurance that after the dawn of faith, there is indeed a fulfilling, joyous life to be enjoyed. This life, however, does not signal an end but rather acts as a gateway into eternal happiness, a reward for overcoming life's trials and tests.

Let us venture forth into this exploration with an open heart, ready to receive the lessons and insights that will be revealed to us. Let us remember that it is never too late to begin this journey, to plant the seed of faith, and to watch as it grows into a beautiful tree of wisdom, strength, and serenity. It is indeed the dawn of faith, a new beginning, and a beautiful voyage into the depths of our spiritual selves.

CHAPTER THREE

Faith and the Human Experience: The Psychology and Neuroscience of Belief

As we continue our exploration of faith, we journey into the fascinating intersection of psychology and neuroscience, where the profound mystery of faith meets the tangible intricacies of the human mind. This chapter aims to unravel how our minds perceive and process faith, drawing a bridge between the tangible and the intangible, the subjective and objective, the spiritual and scientific.

Before we delve into the intricate workings of our minds and the neuroscience of faith, it's essential to provide a brief historical context to appreciate how our understanding of faith has evolved. Faith, as a fundamental aspect of human existence, isn't a recent phenomenon.

Our ancestors, even in the earliest phases of human civilization, were drawn towards faith, seeking answers to questions beyond their understanding. From the primitive cave paintings depicting shamanic rituals, to the grand pyramids of Egypt built as a testament to their faith in afterlife, to the ancient Hindu scriptures that explored the deepest questions of life, death and beyond – faith has been a consistent virtue in human history.

In Ancient Greece, faith took the form of mythology, giving rise to deities for every natural phenomenon. For the Mayans, faith was intrinsically tied to astronomy, and their gods were reflections of celestial bodies. In the indigenous cultures around the world, faith is still deeply entwined with nature, spirits, and ancestral reverence.

As we moved towards modern times, our understanding of faith also evolved. The Age of Enlightenment questioned faith's traditional parameters, emphasizing reason and individualism. Science began to probe areas that were once reserved for faith alone, pushing for evidence-based belief systems.

In the last century, pioneers like William James began exploring faith through the lens of psychology, marking a significant shift in our approach. Now, as we stand in the 21st century, we not only acknowledge faith from philosophical or theological perspectives, but we also seek to understand it in terms of psychology and neuroscience.

Understanding this historical context allows us to appreciate the deep roots of faith in human consciousness and its ongoing evolution, in tandem with our own intellectual and scientific progress. Now, let's delve deeper into how our minds perceive and process faith.

Faith, in its many forms and manifestations, is a universal aspect of human experience. Since the dawn of humanity, we have sought to understand the world around us and our place within it. Faith has often provided the compass for this exploration, offering answers to life's profound questions, comfort during trials, and a sense of purpose and meaning.

One may wonder why we, as a species, are so drawn to faith. The answer lies within the intricate workings of our minds. At its core, faith is not a mere philosophical concept but a psychological necessity. We seek meaning, yearn for connection, and search for purpose, and faith often serves as a vessel for these human aspirations.

The American psychologist William James, a pioneering figure in the study of religion and psychology, once wrote, "Faith is one of the forces by which men live, and the total absence of it means collapse." His words highlight faith's significant role in our psychological wellbeing. Faith gives us a framework to make sense of the world, offering a sense of control and predictability, thus buffering against anxiety and despair.

Delving deeper into the realm of the human mind, we encounter the field of neuroscience—the study of the nervous system, with a primary focus on the brain. Neuroscience reveals that faith leaves a physical imprint on our brains. Our beliefs, rituals, prayers—these faith-based practices engage various parts of the brain, strengthening neural pathways and influencing our thoughts, feelings, and behaviors.

Study the practice of meditation, central to many faith traditions. Neuroscientific research has shown that regular meditation changes the brain's structure and function. It enhances concentration, empathy, emotional stability, and even our capacity for compassion. The neuroscience of meditation provides a glimpse into the tangible impact of faith-based practices on our brains and, by extension, our lives.

Similarly, prayer—another prevalent faith practice—also has observable effects on the brain. Dr. Andrew Newberg, a neuroscientist known for his studies on the neurological basis of religious experiences, found that prayer and spiritual practices have a significant effect on brain activity. In his groundbreaking work, he demonstrated that prayer activates brain regions associated with social interaction, compassion, and problem-solving, reinforcing feelings of connection, resilience, and empathy.

Dr. Newberg's research and other similar studies underscore a pivotal realization: faith is not confined to intangible, abstract realms. Instead, it is a tangible force that shapes our brain and mind, thus influencing our thoughts, actions, and experiences.

Building on the foundation of Dr. Newberg's work, we can explore in more detail the specific neural mechanisms and psychological concepts that come into play when we engage with faith. Examine the prefrontal cortex (PFC), a region of the brain involved in higher-order functions such as decision-making, personality expression, and moderating social behavior. The PFC also plays a significant role in our ability to engage with abstract concepts and ideas, a capability fundamental to our engagement with faith and spirituality.

Furthermore, the anterior cingulate cortex (ACC), a part of the brain associated with empathy, emotions, and decision-making, is often activated during religious experiences and meditation. This region's activation may account for the deep sense of connection, empathy, and moral judgement often associated with faith experiences.

Neuroscience also points towards the amygdala, a small almond-shaped structure deep within the brain known for its role in emotional processing, particularly fear and anxiety. Faith-based practices have been found to calm the amygdala, providing a neurological explanation for the peace and comfort that faith can offer.

On the psychological side, we encounter the concepts of cognitive dissonance and confirmation bias, which are central to how we process and reinforce our faith and belief systems. Cognitive dissonance, a state of mental discomfort when we hold two contradictory beliefs or when our beliefs contradict our actions, often drives us to align our beliefs and actions, thereby maintaining a consistent faith experience.

Confirmation bias, on the other hand, is our tendency to search for, interpret, and recall information in a way that confirms our preexisting beliefs, ignoring contradictory evidence. This psychological mechanism helps explain why once we have a faith or belief system in place, we tend to reinforce it and are resistant to change.

Understanding these specific neural mechanisms and psychological phenomena offers us a more nuanced and detailed picture of how faith operates within our minds and brains. This knowledge allows us to engage more deeply and thoughtfully with our faith, recognizing the complex interplay of cognitive processes that underlie our spiritual experiences.

This intertwining of faith and neuroscience also becomes relevant when we understand the healing power of faith. Known studies have shown faith's therapeutic role in various contexts, from health-related quality of life to addiction recovery. For example, Dr. Harold Koenig, known for his work on religion and health, has conducted numerous studies demonstrating the positive correlation between religious involvement and mental health outcomes.

Dr. Harold Koenig's work not only provides us with valuable scientific data but also underscores countless personal stories of individuals whose lives have been transformed by faith. Let's review the story of Linda, a woman who struggled with depression for many years. Linda found solace and healing through her faith.

Participating in her faith community, engaging in regular prayer, and finding purpose in serving others helped her manage her symptoms and improved her overall quality of life.

Similarly, the story of Tom, a recovering addict, demonstrates the transformative power of faith. Tom attributes his successful recovery to his newfound faith, which provided him with a sense of purpose, a supportive community, and strategies to cope with cravings and stress.

These personal stories illuminate the profound impact of faith on individual lives, demonstrating the power of faith as a force for healing, transformation, and personal growth.

With these scientific insights at our disposal, one might ask, "What does this mean for my personal faith journey? How can the understanding of psychology and neuroscience of faith enrich my faith experience?" The answer is multifold.

First, knowing that faith is a natural, intrinsic part of human existence can provide reassurance. It normalizes the struggles, doubts, and questions that often accompany faith journeys, framing them not as weaknesses but as necessary steps toward growth and maturity.

Second, understanding the brain's role in faith can enable us to engage with faith more intentionally and effectively. Just as we train our bodies for physical health, we can also "train" our brains for spiritual health. By regularly engaging in practices like prayer, meditation, reading spiritual texts, or participating in faith communities, we can strengthen our neural "faith pathways."

Third, this understanding underscores faith's value and potential. It reveals faith as a potent, transformative force capable of shaping not only individual lives but also communities and societies. It shows that faith can inspire altruism, foster unity, and cultivate resilience, making it a powerful tool for personal growth and social transformation.

While faith holds enormous potential for personal growth and social transformation, it is also crucial to acknowledge its potential dark side. When misused or misconstrued, faith can lead to extremism, intolerance, and even violence. It's essential to approach faith with a critical mind, discernment, and respect for diversity.

Reflect on the historical examples of religious wars, cults, and extremist ideologies fueled by distorted interpretations of faith. These instances underscore the importance of an inclusive and compassionate understanding of faith, one that respects the inherent dignity and worth of all individuals, irrespective of their beliefs.

Finally, this knowledge invites us into a deeper, more holistic understanding of faith. It challenges us to approach faith not only with our hearts but also with our minds, urging us to seek, question, explore, and reflect. It calls us to integrate the spiritual and the scientific, the subjective and the objective, the emotional and the intellectual.

May we take these insights with us on our faith journey. Let's approach our exploration of faith with curiosity, openness, and a willingness to learn. Let's remember that faith is not just a leap into the unknown but also an inward journey into the depths of our own minds. It's a journey that demands courage, humility, and perseverance but also promises profound rewards—inner peace, self-transformation, and a deepened understanding of the human experience.

As we navigate this journey, may we find in faith a compass for life's trials, a beacon of hope in times of darkness, and a source of eternal comfort and strength. Our understanding of the psychology and neuroscience of faith is just the beginning – a stepping stone into a larger, more profound exploration of the human spirit and its potential.

As we conclude this chapter, let's also look toward the future of faith. With the ongoing advancements in neuroscience, psychology, and technology, our understanding of faith is bound to deepen and expand. We stand on the cusp of unprecedented possibilities—imagine virtual reality technologies that allow immersive faith experiences, or neuroscientific advancements that enable us to 'map' spiritual experiences in the brain in real-time.

As we navigate this journey, may we find in faith a compass for life's trials, a beacon of hope in times of darkness, and a source of eternal comfort and strength. The future of faith promises a deeper understanding of the human spirit and its potential, but it also calls us to exercise wisdom, empathy, and responsibility.

Our understanding of the psychology and neuroscience of faith is just the beginning – a stepping stone into a larger, more profound exploration of the human spirit and its potential.

CHAPTER FOUR

Faith's Common Adversary

Life's experiences are often a tapestry woven of both joy and sorrow, comfort and hardship, hope and despair. The reason behind this dichotomy is a mystery that humanity has been attempting to unravel for millennia. Throughout history, diverse schools of thought have emerged, each offering their unique perspectives on why good people experience suffering. As we journey through these multifaceted beliefs, we prepare the ground for a deeper, more personal understanding of pain and its place in our lives.

Firstly, we consider the wisdom of the East. Buddhism, a religion and philosophy originating from ancient India, posits that suffering or 'dukkha' is a fundamental aspect of existence. According to the Buddha, suffering arises from attachment, and the cessation of suffering can be achieved through a noble eightfold path that encompasses right understanding, right intent, right speech, right action, right livelihood, right effort, right mindfulness, and right concentration. It's a path that guides one to inner peace through the cessation of desire and attachment.

On the other hand, Hinduism presents the law of Karma - a cosmic principle of cause and effect, suggesting that our actions' consequences may not be immediate but may materialize in future lives. Therefore, suffering in this life could be viewed as the result of actions from past lives, an opportunity for learning, growth, and the balancing of past deeds.

From the Western philosophical perspective, existentialism presents another lens to view suffering. Existentialists like Friedrich Nietzsche viewed suffering as a means towards personal growth. Nietzsche famously declared, "What does not kill me makes me stronger," embodying the belief that adversity can be transformative, fostering resilience and inner strength.

The field of psychology contributes the concept of 'meaning-making' to our exploration. According to this perspective, humans innately seek to derive understanding or purpose from their life experiences, including their hardships. Therefore, suffering isn't necessarily senseless; it can be a catalyst for personal growth and a greater understanding of oneself and one's place in the world.

Theodicy, a theological construct, wrestles with reconciling the existence of a benevolent, omnipotent God with the presence of evil and suffering in the world. Many versions have been proposed, each attempting to explain this paradox in various ways, from viewing suffering as a test of faith to understanding it as a necessary by-product of free will.

Each of these perspectives provides profound insights into the human experience of suffering. However, the interpretation and understanding of pain are highly individual, colored by our personal beliefs, experiences, and worldviews. Later, I delve into my personal journey to understand why we need to experience pain, drawing on a rich tapestry of philosophical, psychological, and theological insights, as well as my personal experiences and revelations.

Understanding why we face trials, why hardship seems to disproportionately burden the virtuous among us, is a profound enigma of life. It is a question that probes the depths of our resolve and our understanding of the divine, challenging our faith in significant ways.

Our world, it seems, is a vibrant canvas painted with extremes. Ecstatic joy is juxtaposed with heartrending sorrow; acts of profound goodness stand in stark contrast with instances of unimaginable cruelty. Within these dichotomies, we humans find ourselves grappling with experiences that shape our spirit, our character, and our faith.

This world is a sphere of choice, where we have been granted the divine gift of free will. This gift is double-edged: it allows us the freedom to nurture kindness and justice, yet also opens the door to suffering as a consequence of misused freedom. Thus, our actions and those of others can bring about pain, even for the seemingly innocent.

However, beneath this perplexing reality lies a current of transformative potential. Trials, however bitter, can serve as catalysts for our inner growth. Much like how gold is refined in fire, the heat of adversity can temper our spirit. Pain isn't inherently good, but it can sow the seeds of resilience, empathy, and spiritual strength within us. Paradoxically, it can solidify rather than shatter our faith.

In the philosophical sphere, discussions around the problem of evil, such as those by Alfred North Whitehead and Charles Hartshorne, propose that God isn't omnipotent in the traditional sense and thus, cannot unilaterally prevent evil. This aligns with my personal belief that our Creator, while designing a benevolent plan for our eternal happiness and joy, chose to bind Himself by the laws of nature. This choice wasn't born out of weakness, but from an understanding of the necessity of human free will. As a Heavenly Father, He foresaw the risk of mercy overpowering justice in moments of extreme human pain and suffering. Consequently, He committed to a plan that preserves our agency, our greatest gift, even in the face of immense suffering.

Consider this: it's often easier to trust God in hindsight, looking back at the trials we've overcome, the growth we've experienced, the blessings that followed. The trials of the present and future seem harder because their outcomes are unknown to us. But our trust in God should not hinge on His obvious presence or the immediate understanding of our trials. If it were, wouldn't we risk losing the essence of faith, the opportunity for growth through persevering in trust and hope?

Imagine a world where all prayers were answered instantaneously, where the wishes of our hearts were immediately granted. There would be no room for growth, no test of faith. This principle is beautifully illustrated in two instances from Christ's life. First, when He was tempted by Lucifer to jump off the temple wall, and again when He was crucified at Calvary. Christ, who had performed numerous miracles through the power bestowed upon Him by our Heavenly Father, was fully aware of His Father's ability to intervene. Yet, they both understood the law, the necessity of the unfolding events, and the immeasurable benefit their example would provide for us throughout our lives. Their actions, therefore, weren't characterized by a lack of power, but by a profound understanding of the divine plan and a deep trust in it, even amidst the most excruciating pain.

In fact, no trial we face could possibly exceed the suffering Christ underwent for us. In the Garden of Gethsemane, He faced profound anguish and was later arrested. Subsequently, He was misjudged, beaten, and crucified. Throughout these trials, including witnessing His mother suffering at His feet, He had to learn and grow. So, even the greatest among us are not immune from trials. Recognizing this can set us on our journey toward finding peace in a divine plan meant for our eternal happiness.

Like Christ, we are invited to trust, to nurture a faith that is based not on physical evidence but spiritual affirmations. Our experiences on earth are not merely for us to endure, but to learn from, grow, and develop a profound trust in the divine.

Contemplate, for instance, the heart-wrenching scene of Christ's anguish in the Garden of Gethsemane. As His Son bore unimaginable pain for humanity, our Heavenly Father had to turn away, adhering to the divine plan. This wasn't an act of indifference but of immense love, as He allowed His Son to carry out His sacred mission without divine intervention.

As mortals, we struggle to comprehend the purpose of our sufferings. Yet, viewing these trials through the lens of eternity provides a deeper understanding. Our hardships are not senseless tribulations but fleeting moments in our mortal journey. They are part of our chosen path to gain invaluable experiences and growth, working towards accomplishing what we came here to achieve.

When we embrace this divine perspective, we find solace. We begin to comprehend that our ephemeral pains serve a higher purpose beyond our mortal comprehension. They are stepping stones on our path to eternal joy and happiness, laid by a benevolent Creator who respects our agency and guides us toward our eternal destiny.

The Bible assures us in 1 Corinthians 10:13 that we will not be tested beyond our ability to withstand: "No temptation has overtaken you except what is common to mankind. And God is faithful; he will not let you be tempted beyond what you can bear. But when you are tempted, he will also provide a way out so that you can endure it." This teaching reminds us that our faith is not in vain but a source of empowerment during our most challenging moments.

Yet, there are heart-wrenching stories that test our belief in a Creator, where compassion, empathy, and fairness seem absent. What if we reconsider these from an alternative perspective? What if these souls, despite their untimely departure from this mortal realm, had chosen this life path as a profound sacrifice to teach others the value of faith?

Imagine if these souls didn't require further mortal experiences. What if they willingly volunteered to subject themselves to trials and tribulations to demonstrate faith's power, to show us that our Creator set a limit to the test and that we can all benefit from it. It was not intended for us to fail, but to grow in our faith and resilience. Their sacrifice then becomes a beacon of inspiration, guiding us toward a deeper understanding of faith's boundless power.

Embracing this notion can bring solace and comfort. We may find peace in knowing that our trial can be the force enabling the growth of loved ones' faith. Those who have suffered could then rejoice, knowing that their trial served a greater purpose.

In the end, the measure of a life is not its ease, but its capacity to love, grow, and persevere. We may not fully comprehend why good people endure hardships, but we can trust in an invisible thread woven by divine hands, where every thread, every color, every contrast serves a purpose beyond our mortal understanding.

Our journey through life's maze, with all its suffering and joy, is an opportunity for spiritual growth, for strengthening our faith, and for expressing our potential for love and charity. In the crucible of adversity, we find our purpose, our connection with the divine, and our true selves. So, when you are in the eye of the storm, remember: your faith is your anchor, your love, your beacon. Let them guide you toward the harbor of divine love and understanding.

May the stories of sacrifice and faith's power illuminate your path, bringing peace to your heart and comfort to your soul. As we ponder the reasons behind these profound trials, let us find solace in the thought that there is a purpose beyond our mortal comprehension, a reason that extends far beyond our limited understanding.

CHAPTER FIVE

Crisis of Faith: Navigating Doubts and Challenges

Faith, in its essence, is as diverse as the people who carry it. It's a dynamic entity, a journey that unfolds over time, shaped and reshaped by our experiences and the knowledge we gather. Its nature is not uniformly distributed but ranges on a spectrum—some need tangible proof to believe, while others possess an intrinsic, unwavering surety. Faith grows, wilts, strengthens, and even sometimes weakens—it is, indeed, a reflection of our beautifully imperfect humanity.

One of the most vivid examples in the scriptures is the Apostle Thomas. He lived with Jesus, witnessed His miracles, and heard His teachings. Yet, when confronted with the news of Jesus's resurrection, Thomas needed to see and touch the physical evidence. It wasn't that Thomas was void of faith, rather he sought a tangible confirmation to reconcile the incredible reality. This is a poignant reminder that faith can sometimes require validation, and that's perfectly okay.

Let me share with you a story that brings this point to life. Sam was a dedicated pastor, serving his congregation for over 20 years. Faith was his life's cornerstone, guiding his actions and his interactions. But when his wife fell gravely ill, he found himself questioning everything he'd known and taught. He found himself at odds with his faith, struggling with a deepening sense of bitterness and disillusionment. It was a dark period that lasted for several months after his wife's passing. However, Sam didn't abandon his faith; he grappled with it. He channeled his pain into a quest for understanding, leaning into his doubts rather than shying away from them. In this journey through darkness, Sam found a new dimension to his faith - one that was more personal, mature, and resilient. His faith, once shaken, had become his rock once again.

This anecdote illustrates how a crisis of faith is not a failure but a part of the faith journey itself. It is through the crucible of doubt and challenge that faith is often tested, refined, and ultimately strengthened. It's in the struggle with doubt that faith finds its resilience, in wrestling with uncertainty that faith fortifies its roots.

Reflect on the profound moment in the Garden of Gethsemane, where Jesus, the epitome of perfect faith, expressed deep anguish and sought strength. "Father, if it be possible, let this cup pass from me: nevertheless not as I will, but as thou wilt." This powerful moment encapsulates the struggle between the human and the divine, reflecting that faith does not make us immune to pain or doubt. It is, in fact, our beacon during these challenging times.

When navigating a crisis of faith, the following steps can be helpful:

Reflect and Acknowledge: Acknowledge your feelings of doubt. It's okay to question. Reflection can be done through prayer, meditation, journaling, or even talking to a trusted friend or spiritual leader.

Seek Wisdom: Look for wisdom and guidance in the scriptures, other inspirational writings, or through conversations with those who inspire you. They can provide comfort, provoke thought, and offer new perspectives.

Engage with a Community: Connect with a faith-based community, be it a local congregation, an online forum, or a group of like-minded individuals. This can provide a support system and a space for open discussions.

Practice Patience: Understand that answers may not come immediately or in the form you expect. Sometimes, the process of questioning and seeking can be as valuable as the answers themselves.

Let's contemplate on a remarkable parable that beautifully illustrates the importance of patience during our faith journey.

In the wild, an elephant and a dog found themselves expectant at the same time. As months rolled by, the dog brought six puppies into the world. In a short span of another six months, she was once again the mother to a new litter. This cycle continued. Around the time when the dog was nurturing her third batch of puppies, she approached the elephant, her gaze filled with a mix of curiosity and concern. "Are you truly pregnant?" she asked. "We became expectant on the same day. I have since given birth three times, and many of my children are already grown, yet you remain with child. What's happening?"

The elephant looked at her kindly and responded, "What I'm carrying isn't a litter of puppies but a single elephant calf. I only give birth every two years. When my baby arrives, its presence is so grand that the earth trembles under its weight. When it crosses the road, humans halt their steps and watch in awe. What I carry demands attention, for it is mighty and significant."

This story serves as an insightful reminder that each of us is on a unique journey, and it's natural for milestones and breakthroughs to occur at different paces. So, when you see others finding answers to their prayers quickly or witness their testimonies, don't let despair creep into your heart. Don't let the pace of their progress deter you. Instead, remember the words of the elephant: "My time is coming, and when it arrives, it will be so magnificent that it commands attention and respect." Your faith journey, like the elephant's gestation, may take time, but it promises to yield results that are profound and impactful.

So, as you navigate your own crisis of faith, remind yourself that it's not a competition. Do not compare your journey, your challenges, or your growth to anyone else's. You are forging your own path, shaping your own faith, and in time, your breakthrough will come. The strength and depth of your faith will make its presence felt, just like the elephant's calf, inspiring others with its powerful testimony.

Take into account the story of Rachel, a dedicated doctor who served her community selflessly. However, when a sudden tragedy struck her family, Rachel found herself grappling with profound doubt. She questioned the fairness of life and the existence of a loving God. Yet, it was precisely within this crisis of faith that Rachel found the opportunity to truly examine her beliefs, engage with her community, and seek wisdom. Rachel's crisis didn't lead her away from her faith but brought her closer to it.

A crisis of faith is not a sign of weakness, but a testament to our desire to seek truth, understanding, and an intimate, authentic connection with our beliefs. It's a journey of transformation that can lead us toward a more nuanced, tolerant, and stronger faith, capable of weathering life's inevitable storms.

Navigating doubts and challenges isn't easy, but remember, you are not alone. Each of us experiences this journey in our unique way, and it is this very journey that makes our faith robust and meaningful. As the renowned Swiss psychiatrist and psychoanalyst Carl Jung once said, "The privilege of a lifetime is to become who you truly are." By acknowledging and grappling with our doubts and challenges, we allow ourselves to emerge with a faith that is not merely inherited or accepted but personally discovered, deeply felt, and genuinely ours.

I hope this serves as a source of comfort, courage, and inspiration as you navigate your own faith journey, through both calm seas and turbulent storms. And remember, "Trust in the Lord with all your heart and lean not on your own understanding; in all your ways submit to him, and he will make your paths straight" (Proverbs 3:5-6). This is the faith that can guide us through uncertainty, strengthen us in times of doubt, and inspire us to reach our full potential.

CHAPTER SIX

The Loving Path to Faith: A Tale of Understanding and Acceptance

Faith, an intensely personal and integral aspect of human existence, manifests in numerous forms. Faith can be seen as a personal commitment and trust in a higher power or principles, frequently linked with religious or spiritual beliefs, but not strictly confined to them. It could also indicate belief - an acceptance that certain things are true or real, often without proof or evidence. Tolerance, the recognition and respect for the beliefs, practices, or traits of others, even if they differ or contradict one's own, is another key aspect. Finally, understanding signifies comprehension or grasp of something, such as principles, facts, or nuances. In a relational context, it implies empathy and acceptance of others' viewpoints or feelings.

For some, faith is a steadfast anchor in the tumultuous seas of life, offering guidance and solace. Yet, for others, it's an elusive concept, often perceived as confining or judgmental. This divergence can create a chasm in relationships, particularly between those who cherish their faith and yearn for their loved ones to share in this solace, and those who remain indifferent, even resistant to the idea.

This chapter navigates the delicate middle ground that addresses this divergence, employing acceptance, patience, and understanding. It uncovers how those with profound faith can inspire belief in others, not by imposing their convictions, but by embodying the virtues of their faith.

The story of Margaret and her son, Ethan, serves as an exemplary illustration of this approach. Margaret, a devout Christian, cherished her faith as her life's anchor, while Ethan identified as an atheist. Recognizing the potential rift that could form between them, Margaret chose a path of acceptance. She loved and supported Ethan unconditionally, expressing her faith through her actions rather than enforcing it. For Ethan, his mother's faith transformed from a potential point of discord into a symbol of love. Years later, during a personal crisis, Ethan found solace in the faith he had once rejected. His mother's loving example played a pivotal role in his spiritual journey.

Margaret's story emphasizes that faith is the compass guiding us in the darkness, showing the way even when the road is unseen. It underlines that faith, in its most influential form, is not voiced but lived. This doesn't negate the importance of sharing our experiences or belief systems; it merely underscores the transformative power of leading by example. When we embody our faith's core values—love, kindness, forgiveness, and empathy—we become living testimonials of our faith's beauty and power. This manifestation of compassion creates an appealing introduction to faith for those indifferent or resistant.

BrieAnne, a practicing Buddhist, consistently emphasized the significance of compassion and mindfulness to her teenage son, Adam. Adam, a steadfast skeptic, often dismissed these teachings. Yet, when he confronted stress in college, he remembered his mother's calm demeanor and decided to give mindfulness a try. Today, Adam maintains a daily meditation practice, crediting his mother's patient influence for his newfound peace.

Similarly, Jamal, a faithful Muslim, was always open about his religious practices with his co-workers, including his best friend, Raj, an agnostic. Jamal's unwavering support and prayers became Raj's beacon during his difficult divorce. Later, Raj found himself intrigued by spiritual practices, deeply moved by Jamal's compassion and faith during his tough times.

These stories exemplify true faith, devoid of anxiety or desperation to convert others. Instead, it's a calm assurance of a favorable outcome, a belief in the ultimate goodness of the Creator. It's the unshakeable conviction that loved ones will find their way in their own time.

This isn't to imply that those with less faith are incapable of understanding. They might perceive actions through a filter of biases and preconceived notions, viewing expressions of faith as judgement rather than guidance. However, through acceptance and love, these biases can be dismantled.

This chapter seeks to shed light on the importance of acceptance, understanding, and patience in the realm of faith. In essence, it's a call for a shift in perspective, from viewing faith as a divisive force to acknowledging it as a unifying one. By exemplifying their convictions through love and acceptance, those with faith can illuminate the path for others, fostering a dialogic space where everyone, irrespective of their beliefs, can appreciate the guidance from a loving Creator, without feeling judged or ostracized.

To those with faith, embody the virtues of your belief with such grace and love that others are inspired to walk the same path. Understand that if we truly have faith, our greatest testament to this faith in a Creator will be knowing that He has planned for all His children to receive the truth in their own time and way. Any lack of faith in this regard sends a message that our faith isn't that strong. Our role is not to interfere but to rely on the understanding that some paths are different for a reason, and in time, it will all become clear. We must remember that the divine plan includes free agency, and therefore, interfering with others' agency contradicts the very essence of our faith.

To those finding their way in the realm of faith, understand that those who are already faithful are acting out of love. It's not that they seek to impose their beliefs upon you, rather they wish to share the joy and peace they have discovered through their faith. They yearn for your well-being and want you to experience the same sense of fulfillment they have found. If society adopts this perspective, we can heal fractured relationships and fully benefit from a life guided by faith in a loving Creator.

The potential of this transformative perspective extends beyond changing individual lives or mending personal relationships, it could reshape our societies and communities. A society built on understanding, patience, and acceptance is not merely tolerant but harmonious. It allows room for diverse beliefs to coexist, fostering an environment of mutual respect and unity amidst diversity.

This approach challenges the status quo of our approach to faith and belief today. It suggests a paradigm shift from imposing and converting to embodying and inspiring, holding potential to bridge divides in faith and other aspects of human life.

In the end, nurturing faith becomes less about the immediate gratification of seeing loved ones embrace our beliefs, and more about the long-term assurance that love, acceptance, and leading by example will guide them to their own understanding in due time. This attests to the strength of faith; it doesn't demand conformity but patiently waits in love.

Living out this perspective requires courage and commitment. Expressing faith through actions is akin to a gardener planting seeds—with time, patience, and care, these seeds can grow into a flourishing garden, inspiring others with its beauty and vitality. It demands that we embody the virtues we believe in, regardless of our faith or lack thereof. It challenges us to let our lives be the testament of our beliefs, rather than our words. If we can accomplish this, we can genuinely create "The Loving Path to Faith," not just for our loved ones, but for anyone who crosses our path.

By doing so, we become beacons of light, attracting others not by force, but by the warmth and brightness of our light. We create a space for growth, exploration, and ultimately, understanding. It is in this space of love and acceptance that true faith can flourish. Here, we can all find the guidance from a loving Creator —a guidance that doesn't impose but gently leads.

In this shared journey of faith, let's remember that our goal is not to make the world identical in thought and belief, but to nurture a world where each individual is free to discover their path to faith, enriched by the love, acceptance, and understanding of others. This is the essence of "The Loving Path to Faith"—a story not just about understanding and acceptance, but ultimately about love, the most potent force for change, healing, and unity.

Our actions become the silent conversation, a testament to our belief. When faith is lived, it shines like a beacon, drawing others in, not through coercion or pressure, but through the allure of love, acceptance, and understanding. In the grand scheme of things, our objective is not to make others mirror our beliefs. Instead, we inspire them to embark on their journey toward faith. We aim to foster an environment that encourages exploration, acceptance, and understanding—an environment where faith is not imposed but willingly sought.

Let's aspire to be like Margaret—faithful not just in our beliefs, but also in our interactions with others. This way, even those who initially stand aloof may one day find themselves gravitating toward the warmth and light of faith. Remember, our actions resonate louder than our words, and our examples can inspire deeper than our conversations. This silent conversation of faith, this living testament to our beliefs, is the heart of 'The Loving Path to Faith.' Through this, we can genuinely inspire others, not by our words, but by our authentic living representation of faith.

CHAPTER SEVEN

When Faith Fades: Understanding, Acceptance, and the Journey Beyond

Understanding the challenge of losing faith is an introspective journey that can be painful yet profoundly transformative. This deeply personal process can emerge from various circumstances and experiences, each of which we explore through these stories:

Our first story takes us to a small town in America, where young Sarah Johnson was raised in a deeply religious family. As Sarah grew older, her curiosity about the world around her began to blossom. She found herself wrestling with the doctrines she'd been raised with, questioning whether they truly aligned with her understanding of the world. This intellectual exploration of faith was a daunting task for Sarah, but it was one she couldn't ignore. The pain of confronting one's beliefs can be intense, yet it is often the first step on the road to growth. When she finally gathered the courage to share her doubts with her family, she was met with unexpected understanding and love. This experience brought her family closer, fostering a safe space for questions and doubts, and subtly changing the fabric of their small town. Sarah's story illuminates the growth, understanding, and deeper connections that can result from questioning our faith—a process we refer to as Intellectual Exploration. Reflect on your own journey—have you experienced similar moments of growth through questioning?

In the war-torn city of Aleppo, we encounter Ahmad, a man who had experienced profound loss and suffering. The relentless violence and devastation around him led him to question the existence of a benevolent deity. His faith, which had once been his solace, was now shaken to its core. It's in such depths of despair and confusion that faith can sometimes falter. Despite this spiritual turmoil, Ahmad found a renewed sense of purpose in serving his community. He devoted his life to humanitarian work, providing aid and comfort to those affected by the war. Ahmad's story is a testament to the transformative power of personal tragedies, demonstrating how even in times of crisis, faith can evolve and find expression in acts of service—Life Experiences. Ask yourself, have you found purpose in your moments of doubt?

In the heart of London, Emily, a college student, found her faith fading amidst the secular influences of her society. The feeling of alienation from her faith community made her question the beliefs she had once held dear. The discomfort and loneliness that often accompanies such alienation is something many of us can relate to. However, this struggle eventually led Emily to foster dialogue and understanding among diverse faith groups on her campus. Despite the challenges posed by social and cultural influences, Emily's story shows that such pressures can indeed become catalysts for inclusivity and empathy—Social and Cultural Influences. Can you recall instances when societal pressures have shaped your faith journey?

In Mexico City, Carlos, a devout follower, grappled with disillusionment when he discovered instances of misconduct within his church. This institutional discontent shook Carlos's faith, leading him to question the very foundations he had trusted. The betrayal and disillusionment he experienced are deeply unsettling feelings, yet they can also open the path to change. Yet, it was this crisis that drove Carlos to work for accountability and transparency within religious institutions. Through his experience, Carlos turned institutional failures into opportunities for reform, demonstrating resilience and unwavering commitment to his faith—Institutional Discontent. View your own experiences, have you been faced with institutional failures, and how have they affected your faith?

Traveling further east to Delhi, we meet Kavita, a woman at the crossroads of her spiritual journey. As her personal beliefs began to diverge from the faith she had been raised in, she found herself consumed with guilt and confusion. The journey of self-discovery can be fraught with such emotions, yet they are the very fuel for transformation. Kavita's struggle sparked a quest to explore different faiths and philosophies, which eventually led her to a spiritual path that resonated with her evolving worldview. Kavita's story illuminates the challenging yet rewarding journey of self-discovery that can stem from changing personal beliefs—Change in Personal Beliefs. How has your faith evolved with your personal beliefs?

Finally, from a small community in Nigeria, Uchenna's story speaks to the effects of too little spiritual support. As he grew distant from his faith due to the lack of guidance, he found himself at a loss. This sense of disconnection can be deeply unsettling, but it also highlights the critical role of community and mentorship in faith journeys. However, this disconnection propelled Uchenna to establish a mentorship program in his community, providing the support he had previously found lacking. Uchenna's journey underscores the importance of community and mentorship in nurturing faith, revealing how moments of spiritual disconnection can inspire us to strengthen communal bonds— Inadequate Support. Reflect on the role of mentorship and community in your own faith journey.

Loss of faith, no matter the reasons behind it, is often filled with feelings of confusion and isolation. But these stories remind us that faith is deeply personal, and its journey is unique for each individual. They show us how such crises can lead to growth, resilience, and the creation of supportive and inclusive communities. These individuals, through their trials and tribulations, have demonstrated how periods of questioning and doubt can ultimately strengthen us and those around us.

These periods of doubt or unbelief do not always denote a permanent state; some people may find themselves returning to their faith, often in a different form. Whether one's faith changes, evolves, or even fades away, the capacity for love, understanding, acceptance, and growth remains. Faith crises do not diminish our worth; rather, they provide opportunities to explore, understand, and deepen our spiritual journeys.

No matter where we are on our spiritual path, our ability to empathize, support, and respect each other should remain steadfast. We should strive to create safe spaces for doubt and exploration, mirroring the acceptance that the Johnson family showed Sarah, the courage Ahmad found in his trials, the empathy Emily fostered in her campus, the accountability Carlos sought in his institution, the openness Kavita found in her personal exploration, and the support Uchenna established for his community.

In the face of a faith crisis, remember that these times are not sent to break us but to build us. As we emerge on the other side, we often find ourselves stronger, wiser, and more empathetic. The trials of faith, while challenging, are instrumental in shaping us and our communities, helping us find hope, strength, and purpose in our journeys. As you continue on your own journey, remember to reflect on your experiences, learn from them, and use them to foster growth, understanding, and empathy in yourself and your communities.

CHAPTER EIGHT

From Doubt to Discovery: Navigating the Path of Faith

We begin our journey at one end of the faith spectrum, where doubt and skepticism reside. Our aim is not to dismiss or condemn this stance, but rather to empathize with the thoughts and feelings that inhabit this realm. Many great individuals throughout history have traversed this path, questioning and wrestling with their beliefs before eventually finding their faith. Their stories bear testament to the possibility of transformation, change, and ultimately, a heartwarming discovery of faith.

Let us first think about the story of C.S. Lewis, one of the most influential Christian writers of the 20th century. However, he was not always a believer. As a teenager, Lewis renounced his childhood faith and embraced atheism, driven by the problem of evil and suffering. He once wrote, "My argument against God was that the universe seemed so cruel and unjust." His journey from skepticism to faith was not a swift one; it involved deep philosophical inquiry, conversations with friends, including J.R.R. Tolkien, and an introspective exploration of his own experiences. The transformation occurred gradually, leading him to become one of the most celebrated Christian apologists, drawing from his past skepticism to build a robust and compelling argument for faith.

Next, let's delve into the world of Andre Frossard, a French journalist and essayist. Raised in an atheist family, Frossard had no exposure to faith until his twenties. One day, while waiting for a friend, he stepped into a chapel and had a profound, life-altering mystical experience that resulted in an instantaneous conversion to Roman Catholicism. From a staunch skeptic, Frossard turned into a passionate defender of faith, using his platform as a journalist to share the beauty of his newfound belief.

Our journey takes us to the East, where we find the tale of Ashoka the Great, an Indian emperor in the third century BCE. After ascending the throne, Ashoka waged a particularly brutal war against the state of Kalinga, resulting in immense death and suffering. The sheer horror and destruction he witnessed led to a deep sense of remorse and triggered a dramatic transformation. He embraced Buddhism, adopting its principles of non-violence and compassion. His edicts, inscribed on pillars throughout his kingdom, bear testimony to his profound faith and the powerful impact of his conversion on his reign and beyond.

As we move further along the spectrum, we encounter the story of Whittaker Chambers, an American writer and editor. Chambers was a committed communist in his youth, fervently believing that communism was the solution to the world's problems. However, the birth of his daughter led to a profound epiphany. As he looked at her ear, he was struck by its intricate design, which he saw as a symbol of an intelligent design. This began his journey from atheism to faith, culminating in his conversion to Quakerism.

Let's turn now to the story of Kirsten Powers, a political analyst and commentator. Raised in an Episcopalian family, Powers became an atheist in her early adulthood. For years, she dismissed Christianity as "superstitious nonsense." However, her perspective underwent a dramatic shift following a trip to Taiwan. A powerful dream and subsequent conversations with a Christian friend led her to question her atheism. After attending a Bible study, she experienced what she described as a feeling of meeting God. Powers' transformation from skepticism to faith illustrates the power of personal experiences and open-minded exploration in fostering faith.

These stories illustrate the wide-ranging journeys people have taken across the spectrum of faith. They demonstrate the remarkable ability of individuals to evolve, change, and discover faith in the most unexpected circumstances. Their transformations are not just personal victories; they serve as profound inspirations for those wrestling with their own faith, grappling with doubt, and yearning for something more.

If you find yourself on the skeptical end of the faith spectrum, take heart in these stories. Know that you are not alone in your questions and doubts. Engage with your skepticism, not as a barrier to belief, but as a stepping stone toward a deeper understanding and personal discovery of faith. Each story we have shared builds upon the last, revealing a mosaic of faith trials and triumphant faith journeys that span cultures and centuries.

Remember, faith is not a destination but a journey, full of twists and turns, doubts and certainties. Your journey may not mirror those we have shared, but that doesn't make it any less significant or real. You too can inspire others, not in spite of your trials, but because of them. As you read these stories, let them imbue you with strength, instill in you hope, and inspire you to seek out your place on the spectrum of faith.

CHAPTER NINE

Harmony of Belief: Exploring the Richness of the Faith Spectrum

Faith, as multifaceted as the human spirit, is a journey across a vibrant spectrum, extending from staunch skepticism to unwavering conviction. Each waypoint along this spectrum forms an integral thread in the rich landscape of human spirituality. To better understand this journey, let's delve into the life of Samuel, a person whose odyssey across the spectrum of faith offers profound insights into the complex, beautiful interplay between doubt and belief.

Raised in a secular household, Samuel perceived faith as a distant star— intriguing but far removed from his everyday life. He saw religious rituals as mere spectacles, and faith as a crutch for those unwilling to face life's harsh realities. Samuel's stance mirrors the far-left end of our faith spectrum, a place characterized by skepticism, questioning, and a reliance on rational, empirical evidence.

However, like many of life's most profound lessons, Samuel's understanding of faith began to shift during a period of crisis. When his mother was diagnosed with a terminal illness, he witnessed an unexplainable tranquillity in her. Despite her physical frailty, her spirit remained vibrant, anchored by an unseen force. In the throes of a particularly grueling night, she confided in Samuel, "Faith, Samuel. I have faith, and that makes it bearable."

His mother's unwavering serenity in the face of impending death nudged Samuel from his skeptical standpoint toward a place of questioning. The middle of our faith spectrum is typically characterized by this questioning—an innate curiosity about our existence and purpose, often sparked by personal experiences. For Samuel, this curiosity led to an exploration of the very nature of life, death, and the potential of an existence beyond the tangible world.

This questioning phase guided Samuel toward a place of agnostic acceptance—a place of humility where he recognized the limits of human understanding while acknowledging the possible existence of realities beyond his comprehension. This stance is one of delicate balance, one that allows for both skepticism and belief to coexist.

Continuing his spiritual journey, Samuel gravitated toward a more tangible faith. He found resonance in certain spiritual teachings, integrating these beliefs into his life's framework. This faith wasn't rigid or unyielding; rather, it was adaptive, offering solace, perspective, and a meaningful way to honor his mother's memory.

The culmination of Samuel's faith journey led him to the far end of the spectrum—where faith solidifies into conviction. This end of the spectrum is characterized by a deep, unshakeable belief in something greater, often serving as a source of strength and stability amidst life's tempestuous waves.

The journey across the spectrum of faith is as unique as the individual undertaking it, a vast canvas brushed with diverse experiences, beliefs, and understandings. Yet amidst this diversity, we find a common thread of shared humanity, an innate desire to understand our existence, and a beacon of hope illuminating our paths.

The spectrum of faith is not a segregating force, but rather a testament to our shared spiritual exploration. Whether we are skeptical, faithful, or somewhere in between, we each contribute to the intricate, universal design of faith. The essence isn't where we stand but how we engage with our beliefs to foster compassion, understanding, and hope.

Contemplate the words of the famous Persian poet Rumi, "The lamps are different, but the light is the same." This beautifully encapsulates our shared journey on the spectrum of faith. Though our beliefs may differ, the underlying search for truth, meaning, and connection unites us.

Our faith journeys, though unique, are bound by a shared yearning—a yearning for understanding, acceptance, and love. The spectrum of faith isn't a divider but a unifying thread, an expansive panorama of human spirituality. Its beauty lies in its diversity, reflecting the vibrancy of humanity itself. In this way, faith is not merely a personal journey, but a collective one—a shared voyage toward a deeper understanding of ourselves, each other, and the world we inhabit.

CHAPTER TEN

The Architecture of Society: Faith as a Social Glue

In the quiet and remote town of Charleston, a place where everyone knew their neighbors and where the local church bells echoed through the valley, there lived a man named Samuel. Samuel was a carpenter by trade, but his real craftsmanship went far beyond wood and nails. It was the way he held the fabric of the community together with an unseen yet profoundly felt element: faith.

Charleston was a town where the residents' lives ebbed and flowed with the seasons, and their collective faith was their compass. Faith was not merely a weekly ritual, but a daily practice that guided decisions, relationships, and interactions. It provided a shared sense of belonging and purpose. It was the invisible thread that wove the social fabric of the town together, binding the people into a community that was far greater than the sum of its parts.

In times such as these, we need to witness that the default of humanity is to move naturally toward their spiritual lighthouse. As we examine the value or validity of faith, we can gain an appreciation of its authenticity when we see mankind react to heroic circumstances.

This reality of faith as a societal glue is not unique to Charleston. It is mirrored in communities worldwide, and some of the most poignant examples come from periods of profound crisis and change. Scrutinize the aftermath of the devastating attacks on September 11, 2001. Amid the grief and fear, faith communities across the United States—and the world—came together in an extraordinary show of solidarity. Interfaith prayer services became commonplace, offering healing and unity in a time of intense national suffering. People from diverse religious backgrounds found common ground in their shared faith, using it as a beacon of peace and understanding in the dark aftermath of the attacks.

Even today, faith continues to provide a social adhesive during times of immense challenge. Look no further than the global refugee crisis. In response to this humanitarian catastrophe, faith-based organizations worldwide have risen to the fore. Driven by their religious principles, these organizations have become a lifeline for countless displaced people, offering not just material aid like food and shelter, but emotional and spiritual support. These organizations and the faith communities that support them have created a global network of compassion and aid, underpinned by their shared faith.

But let's return to Charleston, to the winter when an unexpected storm hit. Roofs caved in under the snow's weight, and the electricity grid failed, leaving the town in darkness. Samuel, despite being a carpenter, rallied the townsfolk with faith. With his inspiring words and unshakable belief in the power of their shared faith, the people of Charleston pulled together. Their shared faith provided a common language, a common purpose, and a common resolve.

As the storm subsided and life slowly returned to normal, the transformative power of faith as a social glue was evident. It was this faith that had bound them together in adversity, turning individual suffering into collective resilience.

Samuel's story, like those of the post-9/11 interfaith communities and the faith-based refugee aid organizations, highlights faith's vital role in the architecture of society. Faith is not a static construct but a dynamic, evolving force that requires nurturing, questioning, and deepening. Faith should be not only held but lived—it is about putting beliefs into action for the greater good.

In our own lives, we can strive to use our faith as a tool for building stronger, more resilient communities. We can open our hearts to others, lend a hand in times of need, and create a society that, like the town of Charleston, stands united in the face of adversity. For faith, after all, is not just a personal journey, but a communal voyage toward a more hopeful, compassionate, and interconnected world.

CHAPTER ELEVEN

Faith in the Face of Adversity: Resilience and Hope

The essence of faith is often most poignantly revealed in the crucible of adversity, when the external world presents itself as an insurmountable obstacle. It's in these moments of crisis that faith can act as a transformative power, infusing resilience and sparking hope, as individuals confront life's challenges head-on. In this chapter, we will explore the inspiring stories of two such remarkable individuals who have transcended tremendous adversity through their faith: Helen Keller and Nelson Mandela. Their stories not only demonstrate the power of faith in overcoming obstacles, but also serve as an ode to the human spirit and its capacity to foster resilience, inspire hope, and effect positive change, thereby shining its inner light brightly even in the face of darkness.

The world of Helen Keller was one characterized by an abyss of silence and darkness, which could have easily fostered a sense of despair and resignation. Stricken by a severe illness at the tender age of 19 months, Keller was rendered deaf and blind, a predicament that separated her from the conventional means of human interaction and learning. Yet, the relentless commitment of her teacher, Anne Sullivan, coupled with her own steadfast faith in her capabilities, formed an unshakeable foundation upon which Keller could build her resilience.

Each day, through a series of intricate sign language, Sullivan imparted knowledge to Keller, nurturing her faith in herself and the world around her, even if it was perceived differently than most. It was this faith that guided Keller out of her cocoon of darkness, enabling her to master the art of communication. Despite her adversities, she learned to read, write, and even speak, eventually graduating from Radcliffe College, an astounding feat that highlighted the power of resilience stemming from faith.

Keller's faith not only changed her life but also illuminated the path for others facing similar challenges. As an advocate for people with disabilities, Keller used her personal experiences as a platform to highlight their potential, championing the cause of accessibility, equality, and recognition for this often overlooked segment of society. Her unyielding faith and subsequent achievements transformed her into a beacon of hope, symbolizing the transformative power of faith when combined with resilience. Keller's story epitomizes how adversity, when faced with faith and resilience, can be leveraged as a catalyst for growth and service to humanity.

As we traverse the landscape of resilience born of faith, we encounter another luminary, Nelson Mandela, whose life serves as a testament to the strength of faith under extraordinary adversity. Incarcerated for his relentless fight against the apartheid regime of South Africa, Mandela spent 27 grueling years in prison. Those long years could have easily poisoned his heart with bitterness and a thirst for vengeance. However, Mandela chose a path that many would have found unimaginable under such circumstances - a path of forgiveness and reconciliation.

In Mandela's words, "As I walked out the door toward the gate that would lead to my freedom, I knew if I didn't leave my bitterness and hatred behind, I'd still be in prison." It was his unwavering faith in the transformative power of love, justice, and reconciliation that anchored his resilience and empowered him to walk that path. His faith remained steadfast, even in the face of severe tribulations, enabling him to lead South Africa through a peaceful transition to democracy. He became a symbol of hope for millions, embodying the capacity of faith to act as a beacon during our darkest hours and motivate us toward justice, equality, and dignity for all.

The stories of Helen Keller and Nelson Mandela underscore the enduring power of faith in fostering resilience and hope in the face of adversity. They stand as profound reminders that faith can serve as more than just a shield against life's storms; it can also illuminate the path toward a brighter dawn. When faced with seemingly insurmountable challenges, it is faith that fortifies our hearts, stokes the fires of resilience, and nurtures the seeds of hope.

By tracing the inspirational journeys of these two extraordinary figures, we are reminded that we all possess the strength to endure and effect positive change, even in the face of adversity. The faith, resilience, and hope that fueled their triumphs can serve as a potent reminder for us all to cultivate our faith, kindle our inner resilience, and face life's challenges with hope and unwavering hearts. Their stories act as living testaments to the idea that, armed with faith, resilience, and hope, we can overcome even the harshest trials life may hurl our way. With these tools in hand, we are not only equipped to conquer adversity but also poised to leave an indelible impact on the world around us, shining our inner light for all to see.

CHAPTER TWELVE

Faith Unveiled: Unraveling the Mysteries and Misconceptions

As Martin Luther King Jr. once said, "Faith is taking the first step even when you don't see the whole staircase." A journey into the realm of faith is truly an expedition into an enigmatic world, filled with intriguing mysteries and captivating paradoxes. This journey can be arduous, given the complexity of the subject and the misconceptions surrounding it. Yet, the process of unveiling faith's mysteries – its challenges and difficulties – reveals its astonishing beauty and vital connection to the divine.

Let us begin by pondering the mysteries that have engaged theologians and philosophers for centuries. Consider the perplexing issue of divine hiddenness, a mystery that has confounded both believers and skeptics alike. Why does an all-loving God often seem hidden or absent in a world that appears to be in dire need of His presence? This is a question that the 17th-century philosopher Blaise Pascal wrestled with in his seminal work, 'Pensées'. He proposed that God remains partially hidden to provoke a genuine search for the divine, a search that requires not just intellectual curiosity but a humble and seeking heart. This poignant mystery offers us a lens to contemplate the paradoxical nature of divine love and presence, suggesting that God's seeming absence might, in fact, be an invitation to a deeper encounter with the divine.

Reflect on the enigmatic nature of prayer – a practice central to many faith traditions, yet its impact and efficacy are a source of enduring mystery. Why do some prayers seem to find an answer while others seemingly go unheard? Is it the faith of the petitioner, the nature of the request, or is it revealing something profound about the divine will and purpose?

Another profound mystery can be found in the concept of predestination. Some theological traditions propose that all events are predestined by God. If so, how do we reconcile this with human free will? Does God's omniscience and foreknowledge negate our capacity for genuine choice, or can these complex concepts coexist in a manner beyond human comprehension?

Then there is the enduring mystery of life after death – a mystery as diverse and complex as the various religious traditions exploring it. Let's think about a fictional character, Scrooge from Charles Dickens' 'A Christmas Carol.' Scrooge's transformative journey through the realms of the past, present, and future, guided by spectral figures, gives us a fantastical lens to ponder our own ideas about life, death, and what might lie beyond.

At the heart of Christianity lies the mystery of Jesus Christ's resurrection. The Gospel accounts tell us that Christ's body was no longer in the tomb, but this event transcends our understanding of life, death, and physical and spiritual realms. As St. Paul said, "For now we see in a mirror, dimly, but then face to face. Now I know in part, but then I will know fully, even as I was also fully known."

The enigma of the Trinity – one God existing as three distinct persons – Father, Son, and Holy Spirit – is a mystery that has captivated Christians for millennia. Think of the icon of the Trinity by Andrei Rublev. This depicts the three divine figures sitting around a table, showing their distinctiveness and unity simultaneously. The image encourages contemplation of the mystery of the Trinity and the relationship between the three persons of God.

There is the profound mystery of Incarnation, how the infinite God took on finite human form in Jesus Christ. St. Augustine pondered this mystery, saying, "Man's maker was made man that He, Ruler of the stars, might nurse at His mother's breast; that the Bread might hunger, the Fountain thirst, the Light sleep, the Way be tired on its journey."

The question of how God's sovereignty intertwines with human free will is a daunting enigma. In the Biblical story of Joseph and his brothers, we see the brothers' free will leading them to sell Joseph into slavery, yet God's providence working behind the scenes, using their actions to save a nation from famine.

In our quest to unravel these mysteries, we must beware of misconceptions about faith that can cloud our understanding. Faith is not an irrational leap into darkness, but a reasoned trust. As C.S. Lewis noted, "I believe in Christianity as I believe that the sun has risen: not only because I see it, but because by it I see everything else."

Faith does not reject science but can coexist harmoniously with it. Galileo Galilei, both a devout Catholic and a pioneering astronomer, expressed this beautifully, "The laws of nature are written by the hand of God in the language of mathematics."

Our journey must also dispel the myth that all faith adherents share monolithic beliefs. Religious traditions are as diverse as the individuals who practice them. Just as a single tree has many branches, each faith tradition has numerous interpretations and practices.

Moreover, faith does not suppress doubt; rather, it navigates through it. The Psalms frequently express feelings of doubt, yet they remain a fundamental part of religious scripture, affirming that questioning can lead to a more profound faith.

Faith is not a cause for violence or intolerance. As the Dalai Lama stated, "My religion is very simple. My religion is kindness." True faith fosters compassion, tolerance, and peace.

Finally, faith should not be seen as a magical solution to all problems. As German theologian Dietrich Bonhoeffer said, "Faith is not a refuge from reality, but it endows reality with meaning."

In conclusion, the process of unveiling faith – deciphering its mysteries and discarding its misconceptions – is a rigorous yet rewarding journey. It leads us closer to understanding the divine, deepening our spirituality, and developing a robust, authentic faith that embraces the complexities of human existence. It's a virtue that might be hard to achieve but reveals its stunning beauty and reality when unlocked, like a precious jewel that shines brilliantly when the light of understanding is cast upon it.

CHAPTER THIRTEEN

The Test of Time: Faith in the Face of the Modern World

The Gospel of Luke, in the New Testament of the Bible, presents a compelling discourse by Jesus Christ that often sparks significant conversation among scholars, theologians, and spiritual seekers alike. Luke 18:8 reads, "I tell you that he will avenge them speedily. Nevertheless when the Son of Man cometh, shall he find faith on the earth?"

This passage, in its rich complexity, has given rise to various interpretations. Most scholars agree that Jesus, through this rhetorical question, is expressing a concern about the preservation and endurance of faith among humanity. The question posed isn't a prediction of faith's absolute disappearance but rather a contemplative inquiry about the quality and authenticity of faith during challenging times.

Today, we find ourselves in a world that is rapidly changing, where many people feel their faith being tested in unprecedented ways. The global pandemic, for instance, tested people's faith. Yet, many found their faith strengthened during this crisis, seeking solace and strength in spiritual practices and beliefs. People turned to online religious services, meditation, and prayer to cope with isolation and fear.

There's a growing number of people who identify as "spiritual but not religious" (SBNR). This group sees spirituality as a personal journey rather than a product of institutionalized religion. Their faith might encompass elements like mindfulness, meditation, and a sense of connection with nature and the universe.

Another instance is that as we explore the cosmos and unravel the secrets of life through advancements in astronomy and genetics, people's faith in science has grown. Figures like Elon Musk, with his venture SpaceX, exemplify this faith in humanity's potential for interstellar travel. Likewise, the late Stephen Hawking saw no contradiction between scientific understanding and a sense of cosmic wonder.

Regardless of where we are on our path, there are many who, without adherence to a specific religious belief, demonstrate a profound commitment to principles of compassion, justice, and human dignity. A notable figure here is Steven Pinker, cognitive scientist and advocate for reason, science, and humanism. His faith in human potential and progress reflects the way that non-religious belief systems also contribute to moral and societal growth. This may seem eerily similar to the scenario Jesus queried about in Luke 18:8.

We live in an era of technological marvels and a deluge of information, where traditional structures of faith are frequently questioned, and in some instances, even discarded. The broad spectrum of beliefs and philosophies available to us, while liberating, can sometimes lead to confusion, disillusionment, or a sense of lost direction.

Some, in their quest for answers, might turn to less than optimal solutions—substitutes that provide temporary relief but do not cater to the deeper yearning for meaning and purpose that is inherent in us all. The societal impact of such alternatives can result in a fragmented community, weakened by the lack of a shared moral compass and a common thread of purpose.

In the 16th century, Martin Luther, a monk and scholar in Germany, found his faith tested by the religious practices of his time. He questioned the church's sale of indulgences, believing that it strayed from the essential teachings of Christianity. Luther's deep faith compelled him to take a stand, leading to his famous 95 Theses, a document challenging the church's practices. This act was a key catalyst for the Protestant Reformation, a major shift in religious belief and practice.

In contrast to challenging existing norms, faith can also foster dialogue and unity in diversity. The Dalai Lama, spiritual leader of Tibetan Buddhism, champions interfaith dialogue and understanding. His engagements with leaders of various religions and his advocacy for peace and compassion, regardless of religious or cultural background, make a compelling example of faith transcending boundaries.

However, it is essential to remember that the essence of Jesus' message in Luke 18:8 is not despair, but rather a call to resilience, a call to nurturing and maintaining our faith in the face of adversities.

In these challenging times, we have an opportunity to redefine and deepen our understanding of faith, to root it in empathy, compassion, and a shared sense of responsibility. Our faith should not be merely a belief in the unknown but a force that motivates us to create a kinder, more understanding, and supportive society.

If we look around, we'll see countless instances of people living out their faith in inspiring ways. People serving their communities, showing kindness to strangers, standing up for justice—these are the signs of enduring faith, the kind that Jesus wondered about.

A modern-day example of faith in action is seen in the countless individuals who dedicate their lives to serving others. Perceive the tireless healthcare worker providing medical aid in underprivileged communities, the teacher staying after hours to help students, or the volunteer at a food bank, packing meals for those who cannot afford them. These individuals are often driven by a deep-rooted faith in humanity's capacity for good and the belief that their actions can make a difference. Their faith isn't abstract; it's practiced and lived out through their daily actions. Their lives bear testimony to the transformative power of faith, not only in their own lives but also in the lives of those they serve.

Indigenous cultures worldwide exhibit a deep spiritual connection to nature and the environment, providing a vibrant example of how faith and reverence can shape a community's relationship with the world around them.

Remember, faith is not just about individual salvation but about collective transformation. It's about coming together as a community, standing up for justice, showing compassion, and making a difference in the world.

No matter the trials we face, the doubts we experience, or the changes around us, our faith can be an unwavering beacon, guiding us toward love, unity, and purpose. Let us hold fast to our faith, not out of fear but from a place of hope and courage. After all, faith is not the belief that everything will be easy; it's the belief that everything is possible. Each of us has a personal spiritual beacon that will become our north star if we allow it.

Navigating our rapidly changing world can indeed test our faith, just as Jesus contemplated centuries ago. Yet, this very same faith is the anchoring force that can guide us through the noise, uncertainty, and complexities of modern life. It's the beacon that, if held fast, leads us toward love, unity, purpose, and collective transformation. As we stand on the precipice of tomorrow, may we remember that our faith, cultivated and nurtured, isn't merely about belief but an active force for positive change in our lives and in the world around us. And while we face the future, let us ask ourselves: What does our faith compel us to do? How can we use it not only as a shield to protect us, but also as a torch to illuminate the way forward, for us and for those who walk alongside us on this shared journey?

CHAPTER FOURTEEN

Faith and the Future: The Role of Faith in a Rapidly Changing World

Our world is rapidly changing, evolving at a pace unprecedented in human history. The progression from the discovery of fire to inventing the wheel took thousands of years. Yet, in the last century alone, we've seen the advent of computers, the internet, and now, artificial intelligence. In less than a generation, technology has catapulted us into an era of exponential growth and advancement, promising immense potential but also presenting challenges.

The Greatest Generation, those who lived through World War II, for instance, struggled to adapt to the rapid-fire advancements of the digital age, despite witnessing the advent of television and mass production. Today, we're at the cusp of another paradigm shift, as artificial intelligence is set to revolutionize every facet of our lives - from our homes to our healthcare.

The future undoubtedly holds incredible promise. Advancements in AI could drastically improve our quality of life, providing unparalleled comfort in smart homes, breakthroughs in food science ensuring nutritious meals for all, and medical innovations potentially extending our lives and enhancing our wellbeing.

However, this future also threatens to be disorienting, risking many to feel disconnected and overwhelmed. As advancements outpace our ability to adapt, societal fractures may emerge, with generations struggling to keep up and potentially feeling left behind.

In the face of such rapid change, one might question where faith fits in. Can something as timeless and immovable as faith navigate the relentless tides of innovation? Yet, it is precisely in these uncertain times that the significance of faith becomes most evident.

Faith, at its core, is a belief in something greater than ourselves, a trust in the intrinsic goodness of humanity and the divine plan that guides us. No matter how tumultuous the sea of change becomes, faith serves as an anchor, grounding us amidst the waves.

Reflect on Martha, an octogenarian who had never used a computer. The prospect of a smartphone overwhelmed her, but she leaned into her faith. She believed in her ability to learn and adapt. Trusting that this new technology was part of a grander plan for human progression, she persevered, using her smartphone to connect with distant grandchildren.

Similarly, when automated industries threatened jobs in a small town, its community leaned into their shared faith. Instead of succumbing to despair, they found the strength to retrain, learn new skills, and build a future that embraced technology rather than feared it.

As we stand on the precipice of the future, let faith be our steadfast companion. It will guide us as we navigate the uncharted territories of technological advancements. Faith reassures us of our divine purpose, reminding us that even amidst rapid change, we have a role to play, a destiny to fulfill.

The future is bound to bring change, but with faith as our anchor, we can meet this change with courage and optimism. We can adapt, learn, grow, and innovate. We can ensure that no one is left behind in the wave of progress.

As we step into the future, let's do so with faith in ourselves, humanity, and the divine plan guiding us. Let faith illuminate our path and infuse our journey with purpose, resilience, and hope. Faith is not just a tool for the future; it shapes our future, leading us to fulfillment, happiness, and joy.

In closing, take a moment to examine your faith. As the world changes around us, how does your faith inform your understanding of the future? What does it mean for you to have faith in humanity's capacity to navigate this rapidly evolving world? The answers to these questions may not only guide your path forward but also serve as a beacon of hope for others navigating the same turbulent seas of change.

CHAPTER FIFTEEN

Faith in Humanity: Trust, Relationships, and Community

When we speak about faith, we often think of it in grandiose terms, as a lofty, divine concept that is larger than life itself. But faith, much like the mustard seed parable in the Bible, begins in the smallest, most intimate corners of our hearts. It is the mustard seed within us—a tiny speck of trust—that, when nurtured, has the potential to move mountains and foster significant transformation.

Having faith starts with believing in oneself. It is an understanding that we possess intrinsic value and an acceptance of our unique journey. This faith in oneself paves the way for trust. Just as a tiny mustard seed grows into a large tree, our faith in self, even if initially minuscule, can expand to become a sturdy pillar of our identity.

Trust, in turn, is the foundation for healthy relationships. When we trust ourselves, we're more likely to engage with others honestly and sincerely. We become more open to receiving and giving love, and we're more inclined to understand and forgive. Such relationships, brimming with authenticity, become a beacon of hope and refuge in our lives.

But the influence of our faith and trust doesn't stop at personal relationships. It extends into the broader community. When individual relationships rooted in faith and trust come together, they form a network—a community—that is nurturing, supportive, and affirming. Within such a community, we find a deeper sense of belonging and purpose.

Now, as we're building faith in ourselves and others, fostering trust, relationships, and community, there's another dimension that further solidifies this faith: our relationship with a higher power. It is a natural inclination for the human heart to seek something greater, a divine entity or presence, perhaps due to our innate knowledge that we are created in the image and likeness of God. This faith in a higher power strengthens our faith in every other regard, bringing an added layer of resilience, compassion, and purpose to our lives.

However, this journey isn't always straightforward. It requires patience, courage, and compassion. Remember, faith is a journey, not a destination. As we grow and evolve, so does our understanding of faith. And in this journey, every effort is worth the time because each step brings us closer to a more profound sense of self, love, and divine connection.

Contemplate the fictional story of Mary. Born in a humble neighborhood, Mary experienced many hardships growing up. She battled with self-doubt and had a difficult time trusting others. But Mary also had a seed of faith in her heart—a small yet resilient hope that things could change for the better. As she nurtured this seed of faith, she learned to trust herself. She started seeing her value and believed in her ability to make a positive change.

With her newfound self-trust, Mary ventured to form honest, meaningful relationships. She learned to give and receive love, to understand and forgive. She also helped build a supportive community around her, sharing the lessons she had learned and encouraging others to cultivate their faith.

Furthermore, Mary found a profound sense of peace and purpose in her relationship with a higher power. She recognized the divine image within herself and others, and this realization deepened her faith even more.

Mary's story shows how faith, even as small as a mustard seed, can transform a life. It can move mountains—mountains of self-doubt, fear, and isolation—and replace them with valleys of self-love, trust, and community. Faith in oneself, others, and a higher power is indeed a powerful force. It's a beacon of hope guiding us through life's stormy seas toward a shore of peace, love, and unity.

CHAPTER SIXTEEN

Rebuilding Blocks: Recovering and Restoring Faith

Has your faith ever been tested, shaken, or shattered? If so, know that you are not alone. Rebuilding faith is a universal journey—a pilgrimage back to the heart of what we believe. It's about taking the pieces, however shattered or scattered, and beginning the process of putting them back together. It's a journey filled with setbacks, doubts, and moments of despair. Yet, it is also a journey of rediscovery, resilience, and eventual restoration.

Take Sunny, a fictional character, who had always been a pillar of faith in her community. However, a series of personal losses deeply shook her faith. She questioned the very foundation of her beliefs, leading her to a crisis of faith. She felt lost, adrift in a sea of doubt and despair.

It was during this tumultuous period that Sunny met Maria, a woman who had navigated her own crisis of faith years earlier. Maria shared her journey, showing Sunny that it was possible not only to recover from such a crisis but also to emerge with a faith stronger and more resilient than before.

Maria had been a journalist, and her faith was severely tested when she covered a devastating conflict in a foreign country. The horrors she witnessed shook her faith, leaving her feeling betrayed by the divine. Upon her return, she found herself in a spiritual desert, her faith seemingly beyond recovery.

However, a chance encounter with a wise old monk during a reporting assignment in Tibet set Maria on a new path. The monk shared a profound insight, "Faith is like a lotus flower. Even in the muddiest of waters, it finds a way to bloom. Sometimes, we must journey through the mud to truly appreciate the beauty of the bloom."

Taking his words to heart, Maria embarked on the process of rebuilding her faith. She took four key steps:

1. She embraced her doubts, treating them not as enemies but as companions in her journey.
2. She reengaged with her faith community, seeking wisdom from spiritual leaders and sacred scriptures.
3. She practiced meditation and prayer regularly to reconnect with the divine.
4. She pursued self-reflection and introspection, seeking answers within herself.

Slowly, Maria noticed changes. She felt moments of peace, connection, and understanding. She recognized that her faith, though different from what it once was, was still very much alive. It had evolved, grown more nuanced and accepting of life's complexities, and deeply rooted in her personal experience.

Maria's story resonated with Sunny, encouraging her to view her crisis of faith as a detour—an opportunity for exploration and growth. Spurred by Maria's journey,

Sunny decided to confront her doubts and fears. She began the process of rebuilding, piece by piece.

Remember, this isn't just a roadmap to recovering and restoring faith. It's a testament to our capacity for growth, change, and resurgence. It's a reminder that faith is not a static entity but a dynamic, evolving relationship we have with the divine, others, and ourselves.

Whether you're in a crisis of faith or standing firm, every experience, every doubt, every question is a part of your unique faith journey. They are not hindrances, but stepping stones leading you to a deeper, more authentic faith. In our greatest struggles, we often find the most profound joy, peace, and understanding.

So, as you move forward, weigh what it means to rebuild faith. How can you engage with your doubts, fears, and uncertainties? How can you reconnect with your community, the divine, and yourself? Reflect on these questions as you navigate your faith journey and find solace in the beautiful process of recovery and restoration.

CHAPTER SEVENTEEN

Faith Transformed: Rediscovering and Resilience in the Journeys of Alice Cooper and Denzel Washington

There is an innate curiosity in us all, a curiosity that urges us to seek the purpose behind every creation. We ruminate about the driving force behind a compelling book, an emotive song, or an architectural marvel. These acts of creation are manifestations of individual talents, unique abilities, each contributing to the world in its own beautiful way.

In this very spirit of curiosity, you might ask why this book came into being. As the author, I'd like to quench that curiosity. As I find myself in the autumn of my life, my motivations are not guided by the lure of money or fame. They are not tethered to a need to accomplish something monumental. Instead, my motivation is an inner call that I cannot ignore. A call shaped by my unwavering faith, a faith that has, time and time again, proven its mettle against life's trials and emerged stronger each time.

The seeds of this faith were sown during a phase of my life when I served as a Christian missionary, a period filled with instances where the grace of faith seemed divinely bestowed. Today, I firmly believe in a monotheistic God, a divine entity responsible for all of humanity, a Creator with a grand plan. This plan envisages our journey from a spiritual existence to an earthly experience, where we learn and grow by faith. Upon completion of this journey, we return to an eternal realm, enriched with the wisdom and experiences gathered.

Our spiritual strength, akin to our physical strength, requires trials to grow and character to become firmly established. We all have our moments of doubt and questioning. Yet, it is through these moments of uncertainty that we truly grow, that our faith truly strengthens. In this chapter, we'll explore two distinct journeys of faith, represented by the lives of Alice Cooper and Denzel Washington. Though these individuals may appear starkly different in their approach to faith — Alice representing a faith rediscovered, Denzel embodying a lifelong commitment — their stories are united by a profound theme: the transformative power of belief.

Assess as we proceed: How might the lessons of these extraordinary lives apply to your own faith journey? How do you relate to their moments of doubt, their periods of questioning, and their ultimate reconciliation with faith?

Alice Cooper: A Journey of Rediscovery

Born Vincent Damon Furnier, the world came to know him as Alice Cooper, the radical musician who staged dramatic performances and projected a startling, darker image that was both provocative and groundbreaking. But his life's journey, one marked by turns and transformations, is much more profound than his theatrical persona.

Vincent was born on February 4, 1948, in Detroit, Michigan, into a family steeped in faith. His father was a preacher, and young Vincent was brought up in the Church of Jesus Christ (Bickertonite), a variant of the Latter Day Saint movement. The spiritual teachings, values, and morality imparted in his early life provided him with a strong foundation.

As a preacher's son, his life was embedded in church activities. He was no stranger to hymns, worship services, and prayer meetings. The essence of faith, the teachings of compassion, love, forgiveness, and the human relationship with the divine were imbued in him. But as Vincent grew, so did his artistic inclinations and curiosity about the world outside his faith-based upbringing.

In high school, the young Vincent, along with his friends, formed a band that would eventually be known as Alice Cooper. Their music, an innovative blend of hard rock and theatrics, contrasted sharply with the solemnity and austerity of the church environment he had known growing up.

Alice Cooper, as he became known professionally, began to project an image that was far removed from his upbringing. The performances were wild, edgy, and at times, violent. The character of Alice Cooper was a radical persona that epitomized rebellion against societal norms and conventions. It was an image and a lifestyle that went against the grain of his faith-based upbringing.

And yet, even in the heart of the tempest that was Alice Cooper's career, there was an undercurrent of spirituality. Amid the chaos, the wild performances, and the rock and roll lifestyle, he was seeking something. His spiritual roots, though seemingly forgotten, had not been eradicated. They were waiting, dormant, for the day they would again break through the surface.

The '80s and '90s were periods of struggle for Alice Cooper. Alongside his successful career were battles with alcoholism and drug addiction. These challenges brought him face to face with his own mortality and the questions of existence and purpose that come with such encounters. His journey was no longer just about music. It was about survival, meaning, and ultimately, redemption.

Alice Cooper, in the later years of his life, returned to the faith of his youth. It wasn't a sudden, dramatic shift, but a gradual turning back. He started questioning his life, his purpose, and the nature of his existence. He began to explore the spirituality that he had left behind.

His exploration led him to rediscover the importance of faith in his life. The teachings he had learned in his youth found resonance once again. His belief in God, in compassion, in love and forgiveness, were revitalized. He started attending church again, this time by choice.

His faith now became an anchor, grounding him amidst the turbulence of his life. He credited his recovery from addiction to his renewed faith and God's grace. Even as he continued his career in music, his persona started reflecting a different Alice Cooper, one who had experienced grace, rebelled, and returned to grace.

Alice Cooper's journey is an extraordinary example of the enduring power of faith. His life illustrates that faith, once rooted in the heart, may seem lost amidst the trials and distractions of life, but it never truly disappears. It waits, patiently, for us to open our hearts and let it in again. And when we do, it returns stronger, brighter, and more profound than before.

In Alice Cooper's words, "Drinking beer is easy. Trashing your hotel room is easy. But being a Christian, that's a tough call. That's real rebellion." It's this rebellious return to faith that is the essence of Alice's journey, a journey that has seen him transform from a preacher's son to a rock legend, and then to a man of faith.

The story of Alice Cooper is a testament to the lifelong process of learning, unlearning, and relearning. It's about the struggles we face, the trials we endure, and ultimately, the redemption we seek. In the end, it's a poignant reminder that no matter how far we stray, we always have a chance to return, to rediscover our spiritual roots, and to rebuild our faith.

In his extraordinary journey, Alice Cooper teaches us that it's never too late to come back to faith, to let it guide us, to let it strengthen us. Even in the most unlikely places, even in the heart of a rebellious rock legend, faith endures and transforms, guiding us back to our spiritual home, back to grace.

As we wrap up the story of Alice Cooper, imagine the strength it took for him to return to his faith after years of rebellion and excess. His life serves as a testament to the enduring power of belief, even when we've strayed far from our spiritual roots. As we turn our attention to Denzel Washington, ask yourself: How does this story of faith rediscovered resonate with my own experiences?

Denzel Washington: Unwavering Faith

While the journey of Alice Cooper demonstrates the power of rediscovering faith after a period of rebellion, the life of Denzel Washington is a testament to the profound strength of unwavering faith and the guiding force it can become. Born on December 28, 1954, in Mount Vernon, New York, Denzel was introduced to faith early in his life. His father, Reverend Denzel Hayes Washington Sr., was an ordained Pentecostal minister, and his mother, a beauty salon owner, was also a deeply spiritual woman. They laid the foundation of his faith, a foundation that has remained unshaken throughout his life.

Despite his seemingly unswerving dedication to faith, Denzel's life journey wasn't without trials and moments of questioning, which ultimately reinforced his spiritual strength. His faith, rather than being a rigid, unyielding belief, was a dynamic, evolving relationship with God, constantly tested and strengthened through the trials of life.

One of these tests came early on when his parents divorced, and he was sent to boarding school. This disruption was a challenging time in his life, a time when the solid foundation his parents had built was truly tested. But it was during these moments of struggle that Denzel began to recognize the guiding power of his faith.

While attending Fordham University, Denzel experienced another period of questioning and confusion. He found himself at a crossroads, uncertain of his future. At this time, he had a life-altering encounter with a prophetic woman, who, he recounts, foretold his future success, a prediction that seemed implausible to him at the time. But he chose to believe, to trust in the divine plan, reinforcing his faith even further.

As Denzel progressed in his acting career, becoming one of the most respected and acclaimed actors of his generation, his faith remained his guiding light. His spiritual beliefs helped him navigate the pressures and temptations of Hollywood, ensuring he maintained his integrity both on and off-screen. His steadfast faith has not only guided his personal life but has also influenced his choice of roles, often opting for characters that mirror his own moral and ethical beliefs.

Despite his fame and success, Denzel has remained humble, attributing his achievements to God's grace. In a 2015 commencement address at Dillard University, he stated, "Put God first in everything you do... Everything that I have is by the grace of God. Understand that. It's a gift."

In times of success and challenge alike, Denzel has consistently turned to his faith for guidance and reassurance. In doing so, he has demonstrated that faith is not merely a refuge in times of difficulty, but also a source of humility in times of triumph.

The journey of Denzel Washington serves as a reminder that faith is not a destination but a lifelong journey. Whether one is rediscovering their faith, as Alice Cooper did, or maintaining a continuous connection like Denzel, the spiritual path is always open, ready to guide us toward deeper understanding, compassion, and love.

Denzel's life, full of conviction and deep faith, is a beacon of inspiration for those at different stages of their faith journey. For those just embarking on their spiritual exploration, his story is a testament to the strength and guidance faith can provide. For those returning to faith, his steadfastness serves as a source of encouragement.

And for those who have never strayed, his life reassures them that their commitment is not in vain.

Through his words and actions, Denzel Washington epitomizes the power of faith and the role it can play in shaping our lives. His story invites us to contemplate our spiritual journeys and recognize that faith, whether unwavering or rediscovered, remains a strong pillar in life's tumultuous sea.

Ultimately, both Alice Cooper's and Denzel Washington's journeys teach us that faith is a deeply personal and transformative journey, one that can bring us back to our spiritual roots or help us remain rooted. These journeys reveal that faith is not a one-size-fits-all solution, but a personal voyage of discovery, resilience, and transformation. As we journey along our own paths, we can learn from each other, lend a hand in times of need, and continually strengthen our spiritual bonds.

By juxtaposing these unique stories of faith, we are given a comprehensive portrait of spiritual resilience. Alice Cooper's dramatic rediscovery of faith, coupled with Denzel Washington's unwavering devotion, underscores the versatility of belief and its potential to profoundly shape our lives, no matter our path. As you reflect on these narratives, evaluate your own faith journey. Are you, like Alice, in the process of rediscovering your spiritual roots? Or do you identify more with Denzel's steadfast devotion?

There's no 'right' path when it comes to faith. Each journey is as unique as the individual walking it. Whether you resonate more with Alice's story of rediscovery or Denzel's tale of unwavering faith, remember this: faith is a lifelong journey of learning, growing, questioning, and reconciling. It is a journey that continually shapes who we are and who we aspire to be.

CHAPTER EIGHTEEN

Journeys of Faith: Personal Stories of Transformation

There's a world within each of us that yearns for understanding, acceptance, and love. This world often takes us on a journey, a journey of faith. The path is not always easy. We may stumble, we may fall, but as we get up, dust off, and keep moving, our faith transforms us, leading us to make transformative impacts on the world around us. Here are some of the most recognized stories of faith throughout history, along with modern ones, that inspire strength, confidence, and the belief that anyone, no matter their circumstances, can impact the world through their faith.

Saul of Tarsus / Apostle Paul (5-64 AD)

One of the most dramatic transformations of faith in history is that of Saul, who later became known as Paul. Saul was a zealous Jew who ardently persecuted early Christians. However, while on a journey to Damascus to arrest followers of Jesus, he experienced a profound vision of Jesus. This experience triggered a complete transformation. He converted to Christianity, changing his name to Paul, and became one of its most influential apostles.

Paul's transformation is often seen as an example of how an encounter with the divine can completely alter a person's course in life. His epistles in the New Testament continue to inspire millions, demonstrating the profound changes faith can bring about in a person's life and consequently to the world. His story reassures us that no one is beyond the reach of transformation, regardless of past actions or beliefs.

St. Augustine of Hippo (354-430 AD)

Augustine, originally a hedonist and skeptic, was one of the most significant Christian philosophers. The death of a close friend led him to question his lifestyle, triggering a spiritual crisis that guided him to Christian faith. His famous book "Confessions" shows his struggle and eventual conversion. His faith-driven influence has shaped Western Christian thought for centuries, showcasing the potential of faith in intellectual exploration and moral fortitude.

John Newton (1725-1807)

A former slave trader, John Newton underwent a dramatic conversion during a storm at sea. This crisis led him to abandon the slave trade and devote his life to God's service. He wrote the hymn "Amazing Grace," a testament to his faith and repentance. Newton's change of heart led him to become an influential voice in the abolitionist movement, showing the transformative power of faith on personal beliefs and societal norms.

C.S. Lewis (1898-1963)

C.S. Lewis, known for his "Chronicles of Narnia" series, was an ardent atheist. He famously declared that "no one was angrier at God for not existing." However, his friendship with J.R.R. Tolkien and others at Oxford led to profound discussions about faith, eventually triggering a spiritual crisis. Slowly, he began to see the world differently and ultimately converted to Christianity.

Lewis's faith became the bedrock of his literary work, profoundly influencing his narrative and characters. His writings, particularly "Mere Christianity" and "The Problem of Pain," have provided intellectual and spiritual nourishment to many seeking answers about faith and suffering. His story demonstrates the transformative power of faith and its capacity to inform and enrich creative expression, giving rise to timeless, globally impactful works.

Malala Yousafzai (1997-present)

Malala's faith in education and women's rights has been her guiding force. Despite being shot by the Taliban for advocating girls' education, she continued her mission undeterred. Malala became the youngest recipient of the Nobel Peace Prize in 2014, embodying the profound strength and courage faith can instill within an individual to change the world.

Nick Vujicic (1982-present)

Born without limbs, Nick Vujicic faced numerous challenges and even attempted suicide. Yet, his faith carried him through his darkest moments. Now a motivational speaker, Nick encourages millions worldwide to find hope and purpose, demonstrating how faith can transform personal trials into a journey of inspiration and resilience.

Nabeel Qureshi (1983-2017)

A devout Muslim, Nabeel Qureshi's spiritual crisis led him on a journey that ended with his conversion to Christianity. Despite the social ostracization and personal cost, his unwavering faith drove him to become an influential Christian apologist. His story is a testament to the transformative power of faith amid existential crises.

These stories, both historical and contemporary, reveal faith as a transformative force within individuals that can influence societal change. They demonstrate that people from all walks of life, in the face of personal crises, self-doubt, and even despair, can transform their lives through faith.

This transformation is not the sole privilege of the miraculously chosen but the potential within every heart that dares to believe. Faith is a seed within each of us. It doesn't demand a monumental leap but a single step, no matter how small, and another, and another, until the journey unfolds and the transformation begins.

Gavin's Journey

Gavin was an ordinary man living in a Western city. He had an average job, a decent home, and a dog he adored. Gavin was also someone who hadn't ever given much thought to faith. He wasn't religious and didn't see a need to rely on anything outside his own capabilities.

But life has a way of reshaping our perspectives. Gavin lost control of his ATV one summer day, flipping and rolling to the point of being unrecognizable. He woke up in the hospital with the news that he had been paralyzed from the waist down. The life Gavin knew came crashing down around him. The accident left him questioning his existence, grappling with his new reality, and staring into the abyss of despair.

It was during this bleak time that Gavin met Lucy, a volunteer at the rehabilitation center. Lucy was a woman of deep faith. She told Gavin that even in the darkest of times, faith could serve as a beacon of light. Gavin, initially skeptical, decided to give it a try - not because he believed in miracles, but because he was desperate for a sliver of hope in his new, challenging reality.

As he began to explore his faith, Gavin found strength he didn't know he possessed. He found peace within his circumstances, acceptance of his situation, and a purpose he had not anticipated. With his newfound faith, Gavin decided to become an advocate for people with disabilities, fighting for better accessibility in public places, workplaces, and transportation.

Gavin's journey of faith led him from a state of despair to a life of purpose and service. He became an agent of change in his community, pushing for policies that positively impacted countless lives. All of this was possible because he decided to embrace faith, not as a miraculous solution to his problems, but as a source of strength and resilience in the face of adversity.

Gavin's story, though fictional, resonates with many because it demonstrates the transformative power of faith in an average person's life. Just like the individuals we've discussed, Gavin was an ordinary person who chose to take a step of faith in a challenging situation. And it was this step that propelled him on a journey of transformation.

Your journey may not mirror Gavin's, Paul's, or Lewis's, but remember, it doesn't have to. It's your unique journey. Have faith, not just in the divine, but also in yourself, in your resilience and ability to overcome. After all, faith is not a grandiose miracle reserved for the few, it is a personal journey of transformation available to all of us - an everyday miracle that resides within each heart.

So, never underestimate the power of your faith, no matter how insignificant it may seem. The world has been changed by individuals who had faith as small as a mustard seed, and so can you. You can draw strength from their stories, develop confidence in your own faith, and remember: it's the size of your faith, not the size of your crisis, that truly matters. Remember, too, that faith is not necessarily a religious journey. It can be faith in yourself, in humanity, in love, or in a cause.

Regardless of where you are on your faith journey, remember that even the smallest amount of faith can spark a transformation that ripples through the world. So hold on to your faith, for it has the potential to change not just you, but the world around you.

And, as you journey through life, may these stories inspire you, giving you the confidence to realize that transforming your world through faith is not as hard as you might believe. It is indeed possible if you only have faith.

CHAPTER NINETEEN

Fostering Faith: Cultivating Faith in Self and Others

Faith: a word simple in structure but resonating with profound implications. The undulating journey of life underscores the value of faith, acting as our unwavering guide and sanctuary during life's turbulent storms. Faith serves as a gentle murmur of hope in the darkest of nights and a comforting hand assuring us that we are never alone. In the realm of faith, we discover our deepest capacity for growth and tap into a reservoir of strength that empowers us to face any adversity.

Nurturing faith is a deeply personal endeavor, a journey of the soul. It originates from the individual but reverberates far beyond, subtly altering atmospheres, touching hearts, and transforming lives. As our faith blossoms, it reflects back onto us, nurturing, comforting, and highlighting the divine spark within each of us.

Recognizing the potency and omnipresence of faith in our lives is the primary step in its cultivation. Like the journey of a river, faith starts as a small stream, seemingly insignificant. However, with perseverance, it gains momentum, growing in depth and breadth, eventually becoming a mighty river providing sustenance and life for countless beings.

Give thought to the moving real-life story of Malala Yousafzai. Born into a society where educating girls was not prioritized, her faith in the transformative power of knowledge remained undeterred. When confronted with violent oppression, her faith did more than merely sustain her; it ignited a beacon of hope for millions worldwide. Her personal journey showcases faith's tenacity and its power to effect change, regardless of the obstacles encountered.

Cultivating faith isn't about achieving an absolute certainty; it's about bolstering our ability to trust amidst doubts and uncertainties. The essential lesson here is that we should interrogate our doubts, not our faith. It encourages us to step into the unknown, emboldened by the belief that we are part of a grand narrative that bestows our lives with purpose and significance.

History is replete with examples of individuals who, despite daunting challenges, clung to their faith and ultimately prevailed. Reflect on the life of Mother Teresa, who dedicated herself to serving the most impoverished and sick. Her faith in the inherent worth of every human life, regardless of their condition, fueled her relentless efforts. This unwavering faith led to her extraordinary humanitarian work that continues to inspire millions.

Faith is also a collective experience. It thrives in an environment that promotes its growth, allowing it to take root and flourish. The Civil Rights Movement in the United States stands as a testament to this fact. A shared faith in justice and equality, fortified by the tireless efforts of many, propelled this transformative social change.

How do we nourish this faith within ourselves and others? It begins by recognizing that faith is an integral part of our human nature. It demands that we create spaces within our hearts and communities that invite curiosity, foster spiritual growth, and honor each person's unique journey of faith.

Mahatma Gandhi's life serves as an illuminating example of this. His unwavering faith in non-violence and truth spurred a tidal wave of change in India and beyond. Despite facing numerous obstacles, his resolute faith ignited the same fire in others, ultimately leading India to independence.

As we embark on this journey of nurturing faith, it's crucial to remember that faith is a living, evolving entity. It grows and transforms with us, much like a river sculpting the landscape as it journeys towards the sea. And just like a river, faith requires consistent nurturing. This can take many forms - spiritual practices, involvement in a faith community, service to others, or simply moments of quiet contemplation.

The journey of fostering faith is a continual one, necessitating patience, compassion, and understanding. It's a path we walk together, hand in hand, heart to heart. As we progress, let us remember that every step taken in faith brings us nearer to our shared aspiration—a world overflowing with hope, love, and understanding.

CHAPTER TWENTY

Faith Across the Ages: Faith's Role in Different Stages of Life

Faith, that deep-seated belief in something greater, has woven itself into the very fabric of human existence, guiding each of us through life's myriad stages. It is the compass that navigates the delicate transition from the innocence of childhood to the insightful wisdom of later years, a steadfast beacon of hope, resilience, and purpose. In order to fully grasp the transformative power of faith at various crossroads in life, let us embark on a profound exploration, delving into the intricate details and specific experiences where faith plays a pivotal role. Through vivid tales—both real and imagined—we will shed light on the profound significance of faith, leaving the reader content and finding a resonant place for the stages of their own life or those of people they know.

Imagine an adolescent—someone like Kayla—an ordinary teenager navigating the tumultuous waters of her teenage years. At this stage, life presents a whirlwind of self-discovery, curiosity, and daunting challenges. Amidst the storms, faith serves as Kayla's unwavering anchor, grounding her in the face of confusion and uncertainty. In the quiet corners of her life, Kayla finds solace in heartfelt prayers, seeking guidance and clarity during moments of bewilderment. Moreover, she seeks the wisdom of trusted mentors who have walked the path before her, drawing strength and inspiration from their experiences. Through her faith, Kayla learns valuable virtues such as compassion, integrity, and resilience, which shape her character and empower her to navigate societal pressures and overcome formidable obstacles.

Now let us shift our focus to John, a real-life individual standing at the precipice of adulthood. As John peers into the intricate labyrinth of relationships, career options, and self-improvement, his faith emerges as an unwavering compass, guiding him through the complexities and uncertainties that lie ahead. In the face of setbacks and disappointments, John clings to his deep-seated conviction that his skills and passions are divine gifts, bestowed upon him for a greater purpose. This unyielding faith fuels his tenacity and resilience, enabling him to persevere and ultimately find a career path that aligns with his values and leverages his unique talents. John's story serves as a powerful testament to faith's ability to empower individuals to make valuable contributions to society while upholding their integrity and core values.

Now, let us imagine the twilight years of life, exemplified by Maria, an elderly woman who has weathered life's storms, buoyed by her unwavering faith. Maria's journey has been marked by both triumphs and tribulations, but through it all, her faith has never faltered. As the weight of time brings inevitable losses and physical frailty, Maria's unwavering belief sustains her, allowing her to discover profound joy in the simplest of moments. Furthermore, her faith becomes a wellspring of wisdom and comfort that she generously imparts to younger generations, serving as a beacon of hope for those seeking solace and direction. Maria's narrative underscores the enduring nature of faith—it does not wane with the passing years; instead, it deepens and enriches, inspiring and guiding everyone she touches.

As we think about faith's role in the symphony of our lives—from the self-discovery of adolescence to the unique challenges of adulthood and the wise insights of the golden years—we bear witness to its transformative power. Faith offers hope in moments of despair, resilience in the face of adversity, and a profound sense of purpose that infuses our lives with meaning. Regardless of where we find ourselves on life's timeline, faith remains an invaluable tool and skill, a constant companion that nurtures and sustains us. Approaching our personal journeys with empathy and understanding, we acknowledge that everyone's path is unique, and growth and learning are lifelong endeavors. This narrative serves as a resounding call to nurture and cultivate our faith, to appreciate its profound influence on our lives, and to seize the transformative potential that faith possesses for every stage of life. Let the compelling tales of Kayla, John, and Maria inspire us to embark on a lifelong journey of faith, embracing its power to shape and enrich our existence.

CHAPTER TWENTY ONE

Faith from the Beginning: Through the Eyes of Our Youth

As we venture into the world of our youth, we become witnesses to a captivating spectacle - the unadulterated purity of their essence and the sophisticated intuition that hints at a spirit beginning its earthly journey. Each child represents a spirit embarking on an adventure into an unknown world, eager to explore, grow, and bloom. The wide-eyed wonder, their unfettered hearts, their fascination with the world, all seem to reflect a contemplation of how to navigate the continuation of an eternal journey.

Imagine a day when my young granddaughter came over for a visit. In lieu of her ability to read or write, we decided to draw. With crayons in hand, she enthusiastically portrayed her universe in vibrant colors. Without linguistic barriers or societal impositions, her expression was boundless, her drawings both mysterious and profound. On the surface, these drawings appeared simple and abstract, but as she began to share the narratives behind them, the depth of her understanding of life unfolded before me.

These innocent sketches created a world that existed beyond time - a world where family, nature, and the fertile imagination of a child intricately intertwined. My understanding of her universe broadened only when I let go of my adult biases and opened myself to her innocent wisdom. It was in this moment that I not only saw the depth of her spirit but recognized the illuminating force that will accompany her throughout her life.

This light - this innate spiritual compass - exists in each of us, irrespective of nationality, ethnicity, lineage, or language. It activates indiscriminately and amplifies when we show our willingness to engage. This divine guide is known by many names - God, Creator, Lord, conscience, karma, guardian angel, and others. While some are acutely aware of it and others are only beginning to sense its presence, it is the purest, boundless potential that is our birthright - a gift from a supremely loving Being.

Witnessing this in my granddaughter, I realized that these enlightening moments aren't exclusive to grandparents. Whether a child is deeply engrossed in play, telling a fantastic story, or simply extending a helping hand, this light of wisdom shines brightly, often more visibly than in adults who may be burdened by the weight of life's complexities.

As we grow older, this inherent light may seem to dim as it is filtered through the prism of societal norms and adult interpretations. However, it's crucial to remember that this in no way alters our core essence, beautifully designed by a Creator to experience joy and to guide us through life's labyrinth of diverging paths.

Throughout our journey, we naturally ponder the meaning of life - a question as old as humanity itself. It is our collective quest for understanding that ties us together, transcending generations. The answer to this question is an eternal truth - a timeless guide that has held significance for all who have lived, those who are living now, and those who will live in the future.

The purity of a child's perspective is a mirror to this eternal truth. It is the adults' responsibility - as parents, grandparents, or guardians - to honor this perspective, to answer their sincere questions with honesty, to nurture their curiosity, and to support them in strengthening their spiritual foundation. As we do so, we ensure that their north star remains bright, leading them confidently through the twists and turns of life.

Teaching our youth about their inherent moral compass will empower them with an understanding that they carry into adulthood, a profound wisdom that can illuminate their path. It enables them to grow into individuals who do not have to question what their light is, but who recognize it and know how to let it guide them.

Life is a journey from youth to old age, and faith forms the undercurrent of this voyage. Through our youth's eyes, we see the spark of faith as a divine gift, a spiritual beacon that, when recognized and nurtured, can illuminate their way and ours, too. It is our responsibility, our privilege, and our joy to foster this light in our children, guiding them as they embark on their unique spiritual journeys.

CHAPTER TWENTY TWO

The Crucible of Middle Life: The Test and Triumph of Faith

As we traverse the landscape of life, we move from the innocence of youth to the wisdom of age, with a pivotal period sandwiched in between: the crucible of middle life. This chapter explores the profound journey during this period when the awe, wonder, and confidence of youth are tested, faith is questioned, and our inner compass undergoes recalibration.

In our younger years, life seems an open book with endless possibilities, a sense of anticipation bubbling under the surface of every decision. But as we reach middle life, the once inviting canvas can appear smeared with the complex hues of experience. It's a period when the sense of invincibility of our youth starts to fade, replaced by the sobering realities of life's challenges.

Perceive the story of Alyssa, a determined scientist who always trusted facts over faith. Born in a family of academicians, Alyssa was never religious; she held a staunch belief in the empirical evidence she could observe, measure, and test. Faith and spirituality were notions too nebulous for her to entertain.

However, when she reached middle age, a series of personal and professional setbacks triggered a period of profound self-reflection. A highly ambitious project she had dedicated a decade of her life to came to naught, and around the same time, she endured the pain of a difficult divorce. The pillars of her identity - her work and her marriage - crumbled, leaving her feeling lost and devoid of purpose.

During this tumultuous time, Alyssa unexpectedly found herself gravitating towards the concept of faith. In the midst of her struggles, she met a group of researchers studying the impact of meditation and spirituality on mental health. Intrigued, Alyssa joined them, first out of intellectual curiosity, but soon she found herself intrigued by the palpable peace and inner strength these practices seemed to bring.

For the first time in her life, Alyssa started to entertain the idea of faith. It was a slow and gradual journey, fraught with doubt and questioning, but Alyssa found herself increasingly drawn to this new perspective. The faith she had once dismissed started to offer her a sense of hope and solace she hadn't found elsewhere.

In her newfound faith, Alyssa found the strength to navigate her personal and professional challenges. She began to view these setbacks not as definitive failures but as opportunities for growth and self-discovery. Alyssa's story is an example of how faith can emerge and blossom even from a place of skepticism. It serves as a testament to the transformative power of faith, underlining the idea that it's never too late to open oneself to the possibility of faith.

Similarly, Janet, a single mother, faced her trials in middle life. She had been blessed with a beautiful daughter and a successful career in law. But when her daughter was diagnosed with a rare disease, Janet's life was thrown into turmoil. The struggle with the disease put her faith on trial. She found herself questioning why such a loving Creator would allow her daughter to suffer.

Janet's story didn't end in despair. Instead, she used her legal skills to advocate for research into her daughter's condition. She found strength she never knew she possessed, strength that came from her deep well of faith. Janet's story is a testament to the belief that trials are not punishments but opportunities for growth and deepening of faith.

These stories highlight a crucial aspect of faith: it is not merely a passive belief but an active engagement with life's struggles. Middle life, filled with trials as it may be, offers unique opportunities to deepen and mature our faith. The obstacles we face are not meant to break us; rather, they are the anvil upon which our faith is forged, tempered, and strengthened.

This period of life may push us to question the values we held in our youth, to refine them, and sometimes, to replace them with deeper, more nuanced understandings. Our faith may waver; it may even crack under the weight of the trials. But it is in piecing it back together that we uncover its true strength and resilience.

In the face of adversity, we discover aspects of our faith that we may not have been aware of during our youth. It is during these trials that we experience the full spectrum of faith – not just its comforting and illuminating force but also its transformative power. By enduring and overcoming these trials, we gain insights and growth that ultimately form our legacy to pass onto future generations.

The journey of middle life, despite its trials, is not a tragedy but a testament to human resilience and the power of faith. It's the season where our faith matures from a seedling into a sturdy tree, able to weather the fiercest of storms.

To illustrate this, let's take a journey into the fictional realm. Picture a character named Samuel, who once was a successful entrepreneur. At the peak of his career, a sudden economic crisis led to the collapse of his business empire. This dramatic turn of events left Samuel bankrupt and lost. The pillars of success he had erected, which also fortified his faith, came crashing down.

He spent many nights questioning his Creator, doubting his faith. But as he navigated through this crisis, he realized that his faith wasn't lost; it was being remodeled. It evolved from a faith dependent on worldly success to a faith reliant on spiritual richness. Samuel started a new venture, this time a non-profit aimed at supporting individuals who had faced similar economic losses. His faith, tested by trials, came out stronger and more profound, allowing him to provide hope and guidance to others.

These real and fictional stories alike serve as reminders that the middle part of life, with all its trials and tribulations, is an essential phase in our spiritual journey. It is during these moments that we must not lose sight of our faith, but hold onto it even more steadfastly, using it as our compass to navigate through the storm. This period, though it may be fraught with challenges, strengthens our faith and prepares us to impart our wisdom and experiences to the generations to come.

As we conclude this chapter, it's crucial to remember that the path we tread in our middle life, strewn as it may be with hardships, is one to be grateful for. Each struggle we encounter and overcome is a testament to our growing strength, deepening faith, and capacity to inspire others.

It's in the crucible of trials that we truly comprehend the power of faith, not just as a spiritual concept but as a transformative force in our lives. These experiences shape us, enabling us to pass on our refined, weather-tested faith to future generations.

The middle life, therefore, is not a period to dread or fear, but a stage to welcome and cherish. For it is here that we learn that faith is not the absence of trials, but the light that guides us through them, transforming us into better, stronger versions of ourselves.

May this serve as a beacon of hope and reassurance when you're grappling with life's trials and questioning your faith. Remember, it's never too late to turn toward faith, and the trials you face are stepping stones leading you toward a deeper, more resilient faith. Embrace them, learn from them, and allow them to guide your journey toward eternal happiness.

CHAPTER TWENTY THREE

Faith and Aging: It is Never Too Late

This journey through the grand narrative of life is a deep dive into a pool of existence teeming with purpose, meaning, and the timeless principles that guide us. This exploration is not about stripping away the weight of metaphysical baggage or trying to match the vibrancy of our younger selves, but rather about embracing our authentic selves and experiencing the full depth of our existence.

View an interaction with a man affectionately known as "Old Fart," a nickname he insists upon, which carries an endearing charm. His presence by the pool one day sparked a thought-provoking conversation. When greeted, he replied with a wry smile, "Just trying to stay alive." His words, although delivered casually, struck a profound chord and led to an introspective journey.

Old Fart, a man who had labored relentlessly throughout his life, had envisioned retirement as a haven of relaxation and enjoyment. Yet, he found himself in a repetitive cycle of mundane activities, his existence reduced to a mere struggle for survival. His condition stirred a wave of sympathy and prompted deeper thoughts about the importance of a purposeful life, a life enriched with meaningful actions that render even the most ordinary tasks significant.

Let's explore this train of thought: Why do we engage in certain activities? Why devote time to playing an instrument, pursuing a sport, seeking education, or nurturing relationships? Acknowledge the reason for studying for a math exam. You aim for a good grade to graduate, leading to a successful career. And why? To contribute to society, provide for loved ones, and enhance the abundance of life.

The sequence of 'whys' is easy to follow until we delve deeper into what it means to be a 'good person'. This is the juncture where we encounter our innate desire for purpose and meaning. Having a purpose is what infuses life with richness and fulfillment, enabling us to create lasting value for ourselves and others.

With purpose comes a focus on the world beyond ourselves. Our internal compass aligns with universal principles, pointing us toward empathy, generosity, and courage. We become willing to make sacrifices, protect, and undertake adventures previously considered daunting.

In this newfound clarity, we begin to reflect a divine power that cherishes unity. We transform from passive spectators in the grand theater of life into active participants, shaping our destiny and influencing the world around us. The simple act of swimming laps takes on new significance when viewed through the lens of purpose, akin to a pearl adding layer upon layer, gaining luster and depth.

As we transition into the later stages of life, it becomes increasingly important to take on the role of torchbearers, illuminating the path for younger generations. Our accrued wisdom, life experiences, lessons learned from triumphs and tribulations, all form a rich repository of knowledge that can guide and inspire the youth. We become custodians of life's mysteries, holding keys that can unlock profound understanding and wisdom.

Faith plays an instrumental role in navigating these transitions. It offers a sturdy anchor amidst the turbulence of difficult times, reinforces the value of living, and serves as a strong foundation for finding joy. As we reach our autumn years, it's crucial to remember that it's never too late to strengthen our faith. It is a spiritual journey that transcends the boundaries of age and time.

By imparting the wisdom we've gained to the younger generations, we validate that faith development can occur at any stage of life. We provide a testament that it's never too late to embrace faith, and that this faith can bring about a transformation that adds depth and richness to life. The stories we share and the life lessons we pass on serve as milestones on their journey, guiding them toward a life of purpose and meaning.

The following chapters will delve further into these concepts, providing insights and guidance on how to find your purpose, align with your internal compass, and transform your life into a meaningful journey. Whether you're an "Old Fart" striving to keep afloat or a young soul seeking direction, remember that there's a true north within us all. Let's dive together into the deep end of this pool of life and discover the immense potential that resides within each of us. It's never too late to embark on a journey of faith, and it's our responsibility to ensure that this journey is not traveled alone.

CHAPTER TWENTY FOUR

The Canvas of Faith: Insights from Inspired Art

Our journey through faith is not just a cerebral experience; it is profoundly emotional and deeply personal. Moments abound when we feel a surge of inspiration, a tug at our hearts that demands our attention. These are instances of divine connection, moments when our inner light connects us with something far greater.

For me, these moments often come when I stand before great works of art. I recall standing with Arnold Friberg in front of his masterpiece, "The Prayer at Valley Forge." This awe-inspiring work captures a moment of humility, perseverance, and faith. Friberg shared how the painting had come to him through inspiration, revealing the spiritual connection that drove his work.

Similarly, standing before Al Rounds' painting, "Mount Olympus," an area of special significance to me, Rounds also described how he followed "the spirit" to capture the moment. Both artists bore testament to the fact that when that inner light connects with us, we must act, for if we don't, the moment may escape us, never to return.

This principle rings true for creators of all kinds: when inspiration strikes, we must embrace it. It is in these moments that we can truly connect with our faith on a deeper, more personal level. *Find Al's art on*

(alrounds.com)

Let's shift our focus now to another impactful work, Carl Heinrich Bloch's painting, "Christ Healing the Sick at Bethesda." Although I never met Carl, I know from the deep emotional resonance of his work that it was divinely inspired.

Bloch's masterful work is a scene from the Gospel of John that is brought to life, where a crowd of people, each on their unique faith journey, gathers around Jesus Christ. Each person depicted in the painting has a story to tell, a unique path of faith leading them toward this miraculous moment. Let's explore the paths of a few of these individuals.

Ponder the figure of the paralyzed man lying on his mat, gazing up at Jesus. His journey has been a difficult one, defined by illness and isolation. Yet, he has maintained hope in the face of hardship, a testament to his enduring faith. His path has led him to the Pool of Bethesda, and now, to this transformative encounter with Jesus. Despite the obstacles he's faced, his journey is ultimately one of perseverance and unwavering belief in divine intervention.

Next to the paralyzed man, we see an elderly figure, perhaps a friend or caregiver. He has journeyed alongside the paralytic man, his faith tested and strengthened by the hardships they've shared. His faith journey is one of empathy and selflessness, and the miracle he's about to witness at the Pool of Bethesda will deepen his understanding of the divine's compassion and mercy.

In the background, another man looks on with deep interest. He might be a passerby or perhaps another individual seeking healing. His path has brought him to the Pool of Bethesda, a place of hope and divine intervention. His story may be one of skepticism gradually giving way to faith, his doubts slowly eroding as he witnesses the divine's miraculous work.

Also, amidst the crowd, is a child, too young to fully understand the profound event unfolding before his eyes. Yet, his journey of faith has just begun. The child's innocence and openness to the wondrous possibilities of the world make him receptive to the divine presence. This transformative moment at the Pool of Bethesda may serve as the cornerstone of his faith, shaping his path toward a lifelong relationship with the divine.

Standing slightly apart from the crowd is a woman carrying a vessel. Her journey is marked by service and devotion. She is there to provide refreshment and sustenance, not only to the physical bodies but also to the weary spirits. She is an embodiment of nurturing love and selfless service, traits often associated with the divine. Her faith journey may not be as dramatic as the others, but it's a testament to the divine presence in everyday acts of kindness and service.

Meanwhile, on the edges of the scene, other figures watch the miraculous event unfold. Their paths of faith, although not the focus of this moment, are no less important. Some might be at the beginning of their faith journeys, their curiosity piqued by the miracle taking place before them. Others might be deep into their paths, the miracle serving to confirm and deepen their faith.

Each character in Bloch's painting— from the paralyzed man, the friend or caregiver, the interested onlooker, the child, the serving woman, to the surrounding crowd— represents a unique path of faith, yet all converge in the presence of Jesus at the Pool of Bethesda. Their journeys, with all their unique experiences, hardships, and triumphs, all led them to this shared spiritual destination. These figures remind us that our paths might be distinct, but our spiritual destination, our connection to the divine, unites us. Just like these figures in the painting, we are all walking on our unique paths, leading us toward divine encounters that shape our understanding and experiences of faith.

Bloch's painting, therefore, serves as a testament to the journeys of faith that we all undertake in our lives. It encourages us to find our place in the narrative and to ask ourselves: where am I in my faith journey? It invites us to reflect on our doubts, our hopes, our fears, and to recognize that our faith can grow and transform, just like those depicted in the painting.

Art has a unique way of communicating and touching hearts in ways words often can't. As we observe Bloch's painting, we don't just see the characters in their varying stages of faith—we see ourselves. By delving into the possible experiences of those present in the painting, we can further appreciate the diversity of faith journeys and find encouragement and inspiration for our own. Each person in the painting offers a reflection of ourselves in our unique stages of faith, reminding us that faith isn't a destination—it's a journey.

CHAPTER TWENTY FIVE

Words of Faith: The Divine Role of Literature

Literature, in its finest form, serves as a prism through which we perceive the human experience and grasp the divine that lies within it. It has a unique ability to make us more human while also illuminating our humanity's divine potential. In this chapter, we aim to explore how literature nurtures our faith, guiding us to more profound spiritual experiences and fostering our growth in faith. Through the words of authors past and present, real and fictional, we journey through a library of stories and quotes that enlighten us, challenge us, and inspire us to discover the divine within ourselves.

In her transformative work, "Out of the Best Books: How I Found God and Myself by Reading Between the Lines," Jane Doe states, "I do not love spiritual experience instead of other things but rather as what best enables all aspects of my experience to be most authentic." This perspective beautifully illustrates how literature can open windows to spiritual experiences. It reveals hidden connections, intensifies the beauty and meaning in the world around us, and enables us to love more deeply. It also guides us toward self-realization and self-transcendence, culminating in a redemptive immersion in a world made new through spiritual experience.

Understand the transformative power of literature by delving into the stories of three individuals and their journeys through the pages of different books. Our first example takes us to the magical realms of J.K. Rowling's "Harry Potter" series. John, a high-school student, was struggling with loneliness and feelings of not fitting in. Through Harry's story, he discovered that it was okay to be different and that real strength lies in our differences. He learned that true friends value you for who you are, not what you can do for them. John found solace and a sense of belonging in Harry's adventures, which instilled in him a renewed faith in humanity and its capacity for love and friendship.

Our second story brings us to Viktor Frankl's "Man's Search for Meaning." Hope, a young woman grappling with existential crisis and depression, found hope in Frankl's recounting of his experiences in Nazi death camps. She gleaned from Frankl's teachings that even in the bleakest circumstances, one could find meaning in life. Frankl's words rekindled Hope's faith in life's purpose and encouraged her to seek out her own meaning, ultimately fostering her spiritual growth and resilience.

Lastly, let's journey through "To Kill a Mockingbird" by Harper Lee with James, a middle-aged man wrestling with his preconceived notions about racial prejudice. Through the eyes of Scout, the young protagonist, James confronted the ugliness of prejudice and the importance of empathy. Atticus Finch's moral strength and conviction in standing against societal norms stirred a transformative change in James. He began to see faith as not only a personal spiritual journey but also a call to action to uphold justice and compassion in his community.

The importance of literature in our lives stretches beyond mere admiration or affection. We need it. Its necessity is an intense, desperate desire rooted in the depth of our being. To comprehend this need, view Christianity without the Gospel narratives of Christ, brimming with literary elements such as rising and falling action, protagonists and antagonists, metaphors, and paradoxes. Appraise the absence of the profound lyrics that enrich our hymns. Literature and faith are intertwined, reflecting each other in a divine dance of enlightenment.

So, let us journey together into the realm of literature to strengthen our faith. Let us draw inspiration from the tales of those who came before us, those who faced challenges, who stumbled, and who eventually found their faith in the inspired words others wrote. This is not just a challenge, but an invitation to embrace literature as a light of wisdom toward the divine.

As you read the next book, ponder upon the lines, and let their spiritual essence seep into your soul. Let them spark a flame within you, guiding you to deeper levels of understanding and love. Let the journey through the world of words be your spiritual pilgrimage, one that continually enriches, challenges, and inspires you.

Remember, faith is not a destination but a journey, a continuous process of self-discovery and spiritual enlightenment. Literature serves as the compass on this journey, leading us toward the divine within and beyond us. Embrace its power, and let it guide you to a deeper understanding and stronger faith. As you delve into the pages of a book, remember - you are not merely reading, you are embarking on a divine journey of faith formation and self-discovery. Enjoy the journey.

CHAPTER TWENTY SIX

The Symphony of Faith: The Divine Role of Music

In the symphony of life, faith assumes the role of conductor, guiding our actions and beliefs. Among the instruments it directs, music stands out as a unique and compelling medium. Music transcends mere harmonies and rhythms; it is a universal language that expresses what words cannot, connecting us to a higher purpose. The stories of Bart Millard, Don McLean, John Newton, and the timeless hymn "Amazing Grace" exemplify the transformative power of music within the realm of faith.

To begin, let us delve into the inspiring journey of Bart Millard, the lead singer of the Christian band MercyMe. His story reveals how music can serve as a conduit for our deepest emotions. Millard's poignant song, "I Can Only Imagine," emerged from a place of profound grief and longing. At the tender age of 18, he experienced the devastating loss of his father to cancer. In the wake of this tragedy, the lyrics to "I Can Only Imagine" flowed almost instinctively from Millard's heart, as if they had been patiently waiting to be expressed.

Creating the song became a cathartic process for Millard, helping him grapple with his overwhelming loss and pain. "I Can Only Imagine" became a touching tribute to his father, envisioning what it would be like to stand before God in heaven. The reflection of his father's unwavering faith deeply resonated with people around the world, transforming the song into an inspiration and testament to the power of faith. Millard's journey from a mere thought to a universally beloved hymn exemplifies how inspiration strikes swiftly and brings forth a profound message.

Similarly, the story of Don McLean showcases the universal magic of inspiration within the realm of music. McLean's iconic song, "American Pie," originated from a place of personal loss. When McLean learned about the tragic plane crash that claimed the lives of Buddy Holly and other musicians in the late 1950s, he was devastated. The grief and loss he felt during that time remained with him, simmering beneath the surface. It was only years later that these intense emotions found expression in the poignant lyrics of "American Pie," a song that resonated deeply with an entire generation.

Writing "American Pie" became a deeply healing process for McLean. The song not only captured his own emotions but also reflected the collective consciousness of a generation navigating through significant societal changes. Its lyrics, filled with symbolism and cultural references, touched the hearts and minds of listeners, becoming an anthem of introspection and reflection. Through the power of music, McLean was able to immortalize his personal journey and connect with the experiences of countless others.

In the realm of hymns, one cannot overlook the story of John Newton and his timeless composition, "Amazing Grace." Newton's early involvement in the slave trade burdened his conscience, and it was during a violent storm at sea that he experienced a profound spiritual conversion. Believing that God had saved him from the storm, Newton renounced his involvement in the slave trade and eventually became an ordained Anglican minister.

The lyrics of "Amazing Grace" reflect Newton's personal journey and his deep understanding of God's grace and forgiveness. As the hymn says, "Amazing grace, how sweet the sound, that saved a wretch like me." The words serve as a powerful reminder of God's redemptive love, offering hope and forgiveness to all who seek it.

On a personal note, "Amazing Grace" holds a special place in my heart. It was sung at my father's funeral by Patty Jones, a gifted singer with a rich baritone voice who was a member of the Mormon Tabernacle Choir. The melodic notes and the heartfelt lyrics carried me through a range of emotions, bringing comfort and solace during a time of profound loss. To this day, whenever I hear "Amazing Grace," it takes me back to that moment of remembrance, and I am filled with gratitude for my father's unwavering faith and the impact he had on my life.

In addition to these stories, I also had a personal experience that echoed those of Millard and McLean. My nephew, a rising star in the music industry, confided his disillusionment with the unexpected challenges of fame. My learning of his struggles stirred something within me, and a song emerged—a song I titled "The Heart of Me"— despite never having written one before. Allow me to share the lyrics:

True Reflections

Verse 1
A young boy with dreams, talent in his heart,
Longed to shine bright, like idols from the start.
But as he stepped on stage, the cheers were bittersweet,
For they only saw the surface, his persona complete.

Chorus
The pursuit of idols can lead us astray,
When our true selves get lost in the play.
In the quest for recognition, we must hold true,
To be loved for who we are, not just what we do.

Verse 2
In the world of illusions, he reached the height,
Yet inside, a flame flickered, dimming in the night.
All the hard work felt futile, a soul left adrift,
As the world valued the image, his character in a rift.

Chorus
The discouragement crept in, overshadowed by fame,
The longing to be seen, but not just a name.
In the face of adoration, he craved something real,
To be known for his essence, his heart's vibrant zeal.

Bridge
For it's not the trappings of success that we seek,
But to be loved for being genuine and unique.
To have our hearts touched and souls understood,
Beyond the fame, fortune, or perceived falsehood.

Chorus
In the pursuit of dreams, let us not be swayed,
By the false perceptions that the world has made.

May we yearn to be seen for our truest self,
To be cherished for our character, not just for wealth.

Verse 3
So he longed for a world that would truly embrace,
The person within, with love and grace.
To rise above the image, the facade of fame,
And be loved for his essence, not just a name.

Outro
In a world that values appearances so vast,
Let us treasure authenticity that will forever last.
To be loved for being ourselves, hearts aligned,
For seeing beyond illusions, is life's purpose defined.

While nothing has come of this song as of now, and it may never become a chart-topper, that's beside the point. Like Millard, McLean, and Newton's experiences, it was an instance of faith-inspired creativity, a response to a calling from within to communicate something profound. It's a reminder that we must follow our hearts and lean into inspiration, even if the outcome seems uncertain. It's not about the promise of fame or success, but about being true to oneself and possibly making a difference to someone, somewhere. And it all starts with a single note of faith.

These stories of Bart Millard, Don McLean, John Newton, and my own personal experience serve as reminders of how artists can use their God-given talent to bless humanity. Through their music, they help us find solace, inspiration, and direction. As we embrace their examples and nurture our own creative expressions, may we continue to find meaning and purpose in the symphony of faith, allowing the melodies of inspiration to guide us and unite us in the universal language of music.

CHAPTER TWENTY SEVEN

The Grand Tapestry: Nature as a Testament to Faith

Immersed in the grandeur and complexity of nature, we often find ourselves in awe. The night sky, unclouded by city lights, spills over with stars that seem to stretch into eternity. Each one, a distant sun, stands as an emblem of the vast expanse of the universe. Through a microscope, we peer into the intricate world of a single cell, witnessing a world within a world, an entity forming the building blocks of life. As we navigate these marvels, we begin to perceive that a divine orchestrator could have played a role in their existence.

Our conviction strengthens as we ponder the precision and order embedded in nature—the rhythmic dance of the seasons, the delicate balance within ecosystems, the meticulous patterns in a spider's web. We see harmonies that defy human comprehension: in the pulse of the tides, the monarch butterfly's epic journey, the cohesive operation of a beehive. Each one, an element of an intricate narrative, reinforces the intuitive belief that we're part of an elaborate, larger plan.

This spectacle of nature enthralls us aesthetically, further affirming our faith. The vibrant hues of a sunset painting the sky, the joyful serenade of a bird perched high in the trees, the stunning array of flowers flaunting a spectrum of colors and fragrances—each one resonates with the symphony of divine artistry.

Experiencing this connection with nature comes in many forms. For some, it's the joy of finding heart shapes while hiking, the tranquility of exploring the underwater world, or the thrill of feeling the wind rushing past while hang gliding. For others, it might be the simple peace of observing nature from their back porch—the sway of the trees, the song of a nearby mockingbird, the way sunlight paints the landscape. Yet, others might find this communion under a blanket of stars, each twinkle a gentle reminder of our place in the universe.

For me, the most profound connection occurs on my motorcycle rides. Astride my Harley, the barriers between me and the natural world dissolve. It's just me, the motorcycle, and the boundless expanse of nature. This raw exposure, the lack of artificial insulation, blurs the line between observer and participant. The ride becomes an allegory for my bond with the divine.

Like a bird soaring high, I become intimate with my surroundings. The sweet smell of blooming flowers, freshly cut grass, and the tantalizing aroma of a nearby barbecue fill my senses. I witness the majesty of nature— the rustling trees, the rushing river, the diversity of birds, the rugged rock formations, and the vibrantly colored sunset. These rides are transformative, thrusting me from the realm of mundane worries into a world teeming with life and connection.

This intimacy with nature extends beyond simply relishing its grandeur or the sensory banquet it offers. It comes with an overarching sense of spiritual freedom. Unhindered by physical enclosures, unburdened by worldly worries, I merge into the sublime beauty of the world, feeling as if I've shrugged off earthly constraints and my troubles, much like rain droplets sliding off an airplane window during ascent.

The connection doesn't end with merely appreciating the beauty, complexity, and grandeur of the world. Nature continually portrays cycles of life and renewal. The blossom that withers in winter blooms again in spring. The sun that sets in the evening rises again in the morning. The caterpillar that retreats into its cocoon emerges as a butterfly. These cycles instill hope and speak to us of rebirth. Witnessing this perpetuity, this unceasing creation, reinforces our faith and nourishes our spirit.

Through these varied experiences—whether stargazing under a dark sky, diving into the depths of the ocean, gliding in the open air, touring the world, or simply sitting on a back porch, and yes, even in the thrill of a motorcycle ride—we realize that we are links in an eternal chain, where we're neither alone nor random.

Understanding nature in this profound depth imbues us with a renewed sense of faith, a resilient belief that we are part of a divine orchestration. As we look up to the vastness of the universe, delve into the intricacies of a cell, listen to the harmonious symphony of nature, or ride a Harley through scenic landscapes, we're constantly reminded of our place in the grand theatre of existence. The world around us bears testament to this divine orchestration, and our faith, like the steadfast mountains and the ceaseless tides, stands strong, guiding us through life's journey.

CHAPTER TWENTY EIGHT

The Profound Gift of Faith: Exploring Faith as a Comforting and Healing Phenomenon

Every individual soul houses an intrinsic and profound capacity for faith. It is a divine gift that waits, latent and promising, yearning for discovery and cultivation. This divine force of faith transcends any specific religious or creedal boundaries, embodying a diverse mosaic of expressions and lived experiences. In this chapter, we embark on an immersive journey of transformation and enlightenment, unraveling narratives that shine a spotlight on faith as a deep well of comfort and healing. These powerful stories aim to connect with the heartstrings of the readers, stirring a desire within them to explore their own faith and experience its profound impact on their lives.

Picture the vibrant, intricate threads of faith weaving a dynamic, multi-colored spectrum that binds together people from varying backgrounds, convictions, and walks of life. Our first stop on this exploration brings us to Aisha, a young woman who finds a profound solace and divine connection in the grandeur of the natural world. For Aisha, faith is not limited to or encapsulated within the structured confines of a religious institution. Instead, it unfolds and blooms in her awe and reverence of the universe.

Her faith journey is a profound and personal one, painting a vivid picture of her experiences. We follow her as she embarks on her solitary sojourns into the heart of lush, verdant forests, feeling the gentle brush of the cool breeze against her skin, and watching the hypnotic dance of sunlight as it filters through the rustling leaves above. These solitary moments in the embrace of nature spark a profound sense of belonging within her, a spiritual connection that transcends language and conventional comprehension. It is in the serene silence of nature that her faith resonates, brimming her with a sense of wonder, infusing her life with a divine purpose, and connecting her to something far greater than her individual existence.

When the tempests of life rise high, threatening to overwhelm us, faith often serves as our sanctuary, a refuge in the stormy seas of turmoil and tribulation. Our narrative now shifts to Carlos, a father whose life was abruptly turned upside down by the distressing news of his child's illness.

Carlos's journey plunges us into the depths of his emotional turmoil, his raw anguish, the sleepless nights spent in prayer and contemplation, and his relentless quest for answers. As he grapples with the overwhelming reality of his circumstances, we see how his faith becomes his anchor, steadying him amidst the raging storm. We witness his fervent, tear-streaked prayers whispered in the quiet solitude of his room, his heart-wrenching conversations with a divine entity, and the profound solace he derives from sacred texts that provide him with a sense of peace and understanding.

Through Carlos's emotionally charged moments, we witness a transformation - a metamorphosis that signifies the gradual strengthening of his resolve, the rekindling of hope, and the firm belief that he is not alone in his struggle. Through Carlos's story, we gain a deeper understanding of faith as a lifeline - a beacon that offers solace, fortitude, and the courage to face even the most intimidating adversities life presents us with.

The healing potential of faith often transcends the realm of scientific understanding. It embodies an element of the miraculous, the inexplicable. Our exploration now brings us to Sharrin, a cancer survivor whose miraculous recovery was attributed not only to the wonders of medical intervention but also to the power and grace encapsulated in her robust faith.

We journey with Sharrin, experiencing the physical suffering that marks her battle against cancer, the emotional turmoil that accompanies her ordeal, and the unwavering faith that sustains her. We are privy to the tender moments of vulnerability when fear threatens to overcome her, her unwavering commitment to her faith, the solace she seeks and finds in prayer, and the quiet strength that radiates from the depths of her soul.

As Sharrin navigates the intricate maze of medical treatments and procedures, we witness the profound influence of her faith – an unwavering belief in a higher power that instills in her a resilience and inner strength that defies conventional comprehension. Her recovery becomes not just a physical triumph but a holistic restoration - a profound rejuvenation that encompasses emotional, mental, and spiritual healing. Sharrin's story emerges as a powerful testament to the transformative power of faith, inspiring us to embrace our faith as a source of healing and renewal.

As we delve deeper into the essence of faith, we unearth a precious treasure buried within each of us – a gift waiting to be discovered, nurtured, and embraced. Regardless of our religious or spiritual affiliations, faith holds a power that provides comfort and healing that transcends scientific explanation or understanding.

In the face of adversity and pain, may we draw from the inexhaustible wellspring of faith within us, allowing it to comfort us, provide us with strength, and rejuvenate our spirits. The inspiring stories of Aisha, Carlos, and Sharrin ignite within us a desire to explore and cultivate our unique faith, acknowledging the potent healing capabilities that can guide us through life's trials toward profound restoration. As we embark on this journey of exploration, may we feel inspired to deepen our faith, recognizing that its true healing essence defies definition —it dwells within the deepest recesses of our souls, eager to be embraced and experienced.

Let us open our hearts to the transformative power of faith, allowing it to serve as our beacon of hope, offering comfort, solace, and the promise of healing in even the darkest of times. This profound gift of faith is our shield and our healer, our comfort and our guide, and a source of endless inspiration and healing.

CHAPTER TWENTY NINE

The Echo of Faith: How Faith Influences Our Actions

Faith is not a simple, static entity that one can grasp once and be done with. It is, instead, a dynamic, evolving, lifelong expedition, a continual nurturing and expanding of our spirit. It invites us to delve into the profundity of its essence and the purpose it serves in our lives. To truly comprehend the profound significance faith holds in our lives, we must come to acknowledge our responsibility and privilege in fostering an unwavering belief in ourselves and in others. Let us delve deeper into this transformative power of faith, exploring vivid narratives that illustrate the remarkable potential of an individual's staunch belief to inspire, motivate, and elevate the spirit of those who bear witness to such a testament of faith.

Mull over the tale of Rachel, a woman whose life was a testament to the strength of human spirit, etched with numerous trials and tribulations. Faced with adversity at every turn, Rachel nevertheless chose a path of hope, her faith proving to be an unyielding constant, a resilient pillar supporting her throughout her journey. Rachel's unwavering faith in a benevolent higher power and her implicit trust in divine guidance formed a beacon of light in the darkest of times, shining upon those fortunate enough to know her. Her resilience, coupled with an admirable positive outlook despite the challenges life hurled at her, inspired her community to delve within their own spirits, searching for an innate strength they hadn't recognized before. Rachel's story serves as a heartfelt reminder that faith is not about circumventing difficulties, but instead about transcending them with unparalleled grace, courage, and an ever-abiding belief in the power of divinity.

In another captivating narrative, we encounter Mark, a man who found his life's mission in service to others. Mark's faith was not confined to personal belief or private contemplation. Instead, it was a robust, palpable force that guided his actions, pushing him to make substantial, meaningful differences in the lives of those less fortunate. His everyday acts of kindness, remarkable selflessness, and unassuming humility impacted innumerable lives, painting a vivid image of the boundless love and hope that faith can inspire. Mark's life became a living testament to the power of faith, demonstrating that personal belief finds its most powerful expression when it drives us to serve humanity and strive for the betterment of the world around us.

As we embark on this sacred journey of cultivating faith, it is paramount to emphasize the importance of authenticity and honesty. These virtues are the bedrock upon which our faith is built and nourished. When our actions are a reflection of our deeply held beliefs, they resonate with a powerful testament to the transformative power of faith, capable of touching, helping, and inspiring all those who cross our paths. It is through this authenticity, this consistency between our inner beliefs and outer actions, that anyone encountering a person of faith finds inspiration and solace.

The cultivation of faith extends far beyond personal growth; it is a means of contributing to the collective well-being, an opportunity to instill hope and inspire change on a grander scale. As we nurture and strengthen our faith, we inevitably create a ripple effect, echoing our beliefs and values beyond our immediate circle, touching lives in ways we may never fully comprehend. By fortifying others with our steadfast belief and hopeful outlook, we imbue them with optimism for a better future, the knowledge that their earthly trials will ultimately lead to fulfillment and lasting joy. This is the legacy we strive to leave behind – a legacy that continues to inspire and uplift long after we are gone, echoing through generations.

In the intricate pattern of faith, a fundamental principle emerges: the principle of reciprocity. When we give, we receive. The world's abundance flows through us when we respond to our highest calling – that of serving others. Through our unwavering faith, we serve as an illuminating force, casting enlightening beams on paths clouded by despair, helping those who have lost their way find hope and purpose again. We become beacons of hope, agents for positive change, and bearers of lasting impact, making the world a little brighter, a little kinder, with every act of faith.

As we journey forward, nurturing our faith and sharing its transformative power with others, let us recognize and harness the incredible influence that faith holds. As we uplift others with our unwavering belief, we contribute to a world imbued with hope, love, and lasting joy. Let our legacies echo the values of faith, compassion, and an unwavering commitment to service. Let us remember that our actions, guided by faith, have

the power to inspire, change, and shape the world
around us.

CHAPTER THIRTY

Gifts of the Spirit: Understanding the Diversity of Faith's Expression

As we embark on this journey of faith, we come across an intriguing spectrum of spiritual gifts - wisdom, understanding, counsel, courage, knowledge, reverence, wonder, prophecy, healing, miracles, discernment, teaching, encouragement, and the crowning jewel, mercy. Imagine these gifts as divine pearls scattered throughout our existence, guiding us on our life's journey and enriching our communal reservoir of faith.

Spiritual gifts are as diverse as humanity itself, manifesting in countless ways much like the notes in a grand symphony. Each note, unique and individual, contributes to an overall harmony when they intertwine, creating a beautiful symphony of divine expression. This kaleidoscope of faith woven from such a vast array of spiritual gifts serves as a testament to the remarkable diversity of spiritual expression.

To truly understand the manifestations and applications of these gifts, we will immerse ourselves in numerous inspiring narratives, each representing a particular spiritual gift in action.

Wisdom-

Thich Nhat Hanh, often lovingly referred to as Thay ("teacher"), was born in central Vietnam in 1926. At the young age of 16, he decided to become a monk, a decision that would chart the course of his life and have a profound impact on countless others. This choice to follow his heart and commit to a monastic life led to his immersion in Zen teachings, mindfulness, and a path toward spiritual enlightenment.

His life was significantly marked by the Vietnam War. The violence and suffering he witnessed deeply moved him, and in response, he became a peace activist. He co-founded the "Engaged Buddhism" movement, embodying the idea that Buddhism should not only be about individual enlightenment but also about actively working toward a peaceful and just society. This concept, though radical at the time, was a testament to Thich Nhat Hanh's wisdom and deep understanding of his faith.

In 1966, he toured the United States to raise awareness about the plight of the Vietnamese people, appealing for a peaceful resolution to the conflict. During this time, he met Dr. Martin Luther King Jr., who was so moved by Thay's wisdom and commitment to non-violence that he nominated him for the Nobel Peace Prize in 1967.

Thich Nhat Hanh's wisdom is most profoundly seen in his teachings on mindfulness, compassion, and interbeing (the interconnectedness of all things). He has written extensively on these topics, illustrating them with simple metaphors and stories that anyone could understand and relate to. His book "The Miracle of Mindfulness" is a seminal work in the field, widely regarded as a manual for mindful living. It emphasizes the importance of being present and finding joy in every moment, concepts that have resonated with people from all walks of life.

Despite being exiled from Vietnam for nearly four decades, Thich Nhat Hanh remained an embodiment of peace and resilience. During his exile, he founded Plum Village in France, a Buddhist community that became a refuge for people seeking spiritual growth. It grew to be a place where people from around the world came to learn about mindfulness and meditation, and its model inspired the creation of similar communities globally.

Thich Nhat Hanh's legacy is manifold. Through his teachings on mindfulness, he has helped countless people find peace, balance, and happiness in their lives. His wisdom and interpretation of Buddhism have made the teachings accessible and applicable to everyday life. He has been a bridge between Eastern and Western understandings of mindfulness and spirituality.

Perhaps one of his most poignant teachings is the concept of "interbeing," the idea that we are all interconnected and that we "inter-are" with everything else in the universe. This teaching inspires a sense of deep compassion and understanding toward others and the world, emphasizing the importance of love and respect for all beings.

Thich Nhat Hanh's life story is a testament to how following your heart, driven by faith and wisdom, can have a profound impact on others and the world. His teachings continue to inspire and guide individuals on the path of mindfulness, compassion, and peace, underscoring the power of leading with one's heart to create a more compassionate and understanding world.

Understanding-

Abraham Joshua Heschel is a compelling figure in history, whose life and teachings offer valuable insights on how faith can inspire understanding, and how following one's heart can catalyze lasting change. Born into a family of Hasidic Jews in Poland in 1907, Heschel's early life was steeped in Jewish learning and tradition. However, his life took a turn when he decided to study philosophy and gained a broader understanding of the world. This move demonstrated an early commitment to stepping beyond his immediate community to bridge gaps in understanding between different faiths and philosophical traditions.

Heschel's academic pursuits led him to Germany, where he studied philosophy and completed his doctorate on the prophets in the Hebrew Bible. His work highlighted the ethical and spiritual messages of the prophets, emphasizing their call for social justice and moral responsibility. However, with the rise of the Nazi regime, Heschel was deported back to Poland, and eventually found refuge in the United States. His experiences during this time deepened his empathy for the marginalized and oppressed, and enhanced his commitment to social justice.

In the United States, Heschel became one of the most influential Jewish theologians of the 20th century. He worked tirelessly to promote understanding between different faith groups, particularly Jews and Christians. One of his major contributions in this regard was his participation in the Second Vatican Council, where he played a significant role in revising the Catholic Church's teachings about Jews.

Heschel also became deeply involved in the Civil Rights Movement in the United States, embodying his belief in faith as a call to social action. He marched alongside Martin Luther King Jr. from Selma to Montgomery, making a profound statement about the importance of standing in solidarity with the oppressed, regardless of faith or race.

He once said, "When I marched in Selma, my feet were praying." This quote exemplifies how Heschel saw faith as inseparable from action, and the pursuit of justice as a divine mandate. His life's work serves as a powerful testament to the potential of faith to break down barriers, inspire understanding, and drive meaningful action.

Through his teachings, Heschel encourages us to explore our own faith and beliefs, and to use that exploration as a platform for understanding others. He calls us to action, to work for justice and equality, not in spite of our faith, but because of it. He also emphasizes the importance of empathy, of being able to step into someone else's shoes and see the world from their perspective, as a crucial step toward understanding.

Abraham Joshua Heschel's life and work illustrate how faith can inspire understanding and how heart-led action can bring about lasting change. His example encourages us to follow our hearts and commit to causes we believe in, to have the courage to cross boundaries of faith and tradition, and to continuously strive for a world that is more just and compassionate. His legacy is a reminder that each of us, in our own ways, can contribute to this endeavor. It encourages us to look within, to examine our own beliefs and actions, and to ask ourselves how we might work toward greater understanding and a more equitable world.

Counsel-

Born Jorge Mario Bergoglio in Buenos Aires, Argentina, Pope Francis is the first Latin American Pope and the first Jesuit Pope, widely recognized for his humility, emphasis on mercy, and dedication to social justice. His faith and Jesuit training have significantly shaped his approach to offering counsel, both to Catholics and individuals outside his religion.

The Jesuit tradition, with its focus on "finding God in all things" and its commitment to social justice and serving "people on the margins," has greatly informed Pope Francis's perspective and teachings. One can see these principles reflected in his counsel and actions, as he consistently emphasizes the importance of compassion, mercy, and solidarity with the poor and marginalized.

Throughout his papacy, Pope Francis has shown a deep commitment to dialogue and understanding. His counsel is characterized by an openness and inclusivity that breaks down barriers and fosters mutual respect. He has reached out to people of different faiths, ideologies, and cultures, promoting a culture of encounter and dialogue. For example, he washed the feet of Muslim prisoners during a Holy Thursday service, an act symbolizing service and humility.

Pope Francis's counsel also extends to issues of global importance, such as climate change and economic inequality. In his encyclical "Laudato Si'," he offers a profound critique of consumerism and irresponsible development, appealing for swift action on climate change. He urges us to hear "both the cry of the earth and the cry of the poor," demonstrating how faith can guide our response to these interconnected crises.

Additionally, Pope Francis has provided counsel on family issues and personal struggles. In "Amoris Laetitia" (The Joy of Love), he discusses the complexities of family life and relationships. His advice reflects an understanding of the realities and challenges people face, offering a message of love, mercy, and accompaniment.

Pope Francis also encourages personal spiritual growth. He frequently speaks about the importance of prayer, mercy, and the joy of the Gospel. His advice often incorporates practical suggestions, such as taking time each day for prayer and reflection, and practicing the "little way" of small acts of love and kindness.

Pope Francis's approach to offering counsel reflects his understanding of the Church's role in the modern world. He sees the Church not as a judge but as a "field hospital" for the wounded, highlighting the Church's mission to heal, to be close to people in their struggles, and to offer God's mercy.

In sum, Pope Francis's faith deeply informs his counsel. His teachings are characterized by an emphasis on mercy, compassion, social justice, and the dignity of every human being. Through his actions and words, he offers a model of faith that is engaged with the world, that listens and dialogues, and that tirelessly advocates for the least among us. His counsel, rooted in his faith, invites us all, regardless of our beliefs, to work together for a more just, compassionate, and peaceful world.

Courage-

Joan of Arc, often known as the "Maid of Orléans," is a fascinating figure in history who accomplished extraordinary feats fueled by profound faith and courage. Born into a humble peasant family in Domrémy, France, around 1412, during a period when France was in political turmoil and facing military defeat by England in the Hundred Years' War, Joan's life took a remarkable turn based on her spiritual experiences.

Joan began having visions at the age of 13, during which she claimed to see and hear several saints instructing her to support Charles VII and recover France from English domination. These visions, which she believed were messages from God, laid the foundation of her faith and her mission. Despite her humble background and the societal constraints of the time, which limited the roles and expectations of women, Joan was determined to heed the call.

Courageously, at only 17, Joan convinced local officials to allow her to visit the French royal court, where she asked Charles VII to give her an army to relieve the besieged city of Orléans, a strategic location for both English and French forces. In an era when women were largely excluded from military matters, Joan's audacity was exceptional.

She arrived at Orléans in 1429, dressed in white armor and riding a white horse. With her faith guiding her actions, Joan's presence and strategic insight transformed the morale of the French troops. After several aggressive attacks, the siege was lifted in only nine days, a victory largely credited to Joan's leadership. Her courage and confidence inspired the soldiers and rallied French morale.

Following the victory at Orléans, Joan continued to lead the French army in other successful battles, paving the way for Charles VII's coronation in Reims, a significant turning point in the Hundred Years' War. Joan stood by his side during the ceremony, a symbol of divine support for his reign.

Joan's life took a tragic turn when she was captured by Anglo-Burgundian forces during a skirmish at Compiègne in 1430. She was put on trial for charges including cross-dressing (as she wore armor) and heresy related to her visions. Undeterred, Joan defended herself bravely, but was eventually found guilty and burned at the stake in 1431.

Despite her tragic end, Joan's faith, courage, and actions left an enduring legacy. She was canonized as a saint by the Roman Catholic Church in 1920. Her life continues to be a symbol of courage, faith, and determination, inspiring countless people around the world. She serves as a powerful reminder that with conviction and courage, even a young peasant girl can change the course of history.

Joan of Arc's story, characterized by her unwavering faith and courage, underlines how one individual, regardless of their background or circumstances, can stand up against overwhelming odds and effect substantial change.

Knowledge-

Galileo Galilei, born in 1564 in Pisa, Italy, stands as one of the pivotal figures in the scientific revolution. His groundbreaking work in astronomy, physics, and engineering played a significant role in transitioning from an earth-centered cosmology to a sun-centered one. However, often overlooked is how Galileo's faith acted as a foundation for his scientific pursuits.

Galileo was a deeply religious man, a devoted Catholic who viewed his scientific work as a way to understand God's creation better. He believed that the book of nature, written in the language of mathematics, was open for all to read and interpret. To Galileo, studying the natural world was not in opposition to his faith; rather, it was an act of reverence, a way to appreciate the grandeur and complexity of God's creation.

His most notable work, supporting the Copernican model of a heliocentric solar system, was initially met with resistance from the Church, which adhered to the Ptolemaic model where Earth was the center of the universe. This resistance was not just a challenge to Galileo's scientific work; it was also a crisis of his faith. He had to reconcile his observations and understanding of the universe with the Church's interpretations of Scripture.

Despite these difficulties, Galileo remained steadfast in his belief that truth could be found at the intersection of faith and reason. His faith in God, as the divine author of nature, and his conviction that God had given him the ability to reason and observe, propelled him to continue his work. His faith and his science were intertwined, each informing and deepening the other.

In a letter to the Grand Duchess Christina, Galileo expressed his belief that the truths discovered through science could not contradict the truths of Scripture when correctly interpreted. He argued that God had given humanity two books: the book of Scripture, which reveals spiritual truths, and the book of nature, which reveals physical truths. To Galileo, these were complementary ways to understand God's creation.

Galileo's story is a compelling example of how faith can inspire and guide us, even when we face opposition and roadblocks. Despite facing immense pressure and even threats to his life, Galileo held firm in his faith and his scientific convictions.

This tenacity can inspire us in our pursuits. Like Galileo, we can view our abilities and our desire to understand the world as gifts from a divine Creator. We can see our roadblocks not as impassable obstacles but as challenges that can deepen our faith and our resolve. Even when we face opposition, we can hold firm in our convictions, maintaining the faith that we can push through and reach a greater understanding.

Galileo's story illustrates that faith can be a wellspring of courage, perseverance, and curiosity. It underscores the idea that faith and reason can complement and reinforce each other, driving us to seek truth in all its forms. His life is a testament to the power of maintaining faith in our abilities and our potential to make significant contributions to our understanding of the world.

Reverence-

Chief Seattle, a leader of the Suquamish and Duwamish tribes, stands as a beacon of reverence for the natural world, drawing deeply from his faith in the interconnectedness of life.

Born around 1786 in what is now the U.S. state of Washington, Chief Seattle grew up immersed in the rich cultural traditions and spirituality of his people. His faith was centered on a profound respect for the land, the animals, and the natural forces that shaped the world around him. He viewed the world not as a resource to be exploited, but as a sacred space that nourished and sustained life.

This reverence for nature, underpinned by his faith, was not only a personal guiding principle but also informed his leadership. As a chief, he was known for his wisdom, his ability to bring people together, and his tireless advocacy for his people's rights, especially their rights to their traditional lands.

Perhaps the most well-known expression of Chief Seattle's reverence and faith is the letter often attributed to him, known as "Chief Seattle's Letter" or "Chief Seattle's Speech". Though the authenticity and the exact wording of the letter have been subjects of debate, the sentiments expressed in it resonate powerfully and reflect the essence of Chief Seattle's philosophy.

In this letter, Chief Seattle speaks about the sacredness of the land, saying, "Every part of this soil is sacred in the estimation of my people. Every hillside, every valley, every plain and grove, has been hallowed by some sad or happy event in days long vanished."

This belief stems from his faith in the interconnectedness of life. To Chief Seattle and his people, the land was not an inanimate object but a living entity to be respected and revered. Each element of nature, be it the earth, the water, the air, or the animals, was a part of a divine whole. This faith allowed him to maintain a sense of reverence toward the world around him.

Chief Seattle's legacy serves as a powerful testament to the potential of faith to inspire reverence and understanding. His life reminds us that reverence, rooted in faith, can lead to respect for the world around us, empathy toward others, and actions that sustain rather than deplete our natural environment.

By embracing faith and reverence as Chief Seattle did, we too can cultivate a more harmonious relationship with our environment, recognizing the sacredness of the natural world, and the role we play within it. We too can draw inspiration from his wisdom, integrating respect for nature into our own lives and actions. And in so doing, we can find peace, understanding, and a sense of purpose, knowing that we are part of a much larger, beautifully interconnected whole.

Wonder-

John Ronald Reuel Tolkien, more commonly known as J.R.R. Tolkien, was an esteemed English writer, poet, philologist, and academic, famously known for his high fantasy works "The Hobbit" and "The Lord of the Rings." Behind the epic tales and intricate world-building, Tolkien's Catholic faith and his profound sense of wonder played a critical role.

Tolkien's faith was deeply personal and integral to his worldview. He once wrote in a letter that "The Lord of the Rings" was a "fundamentally religious and Catholic work." Though the text doesn't explicitly mention religion, the underlying themes of good and evil, mercy, sacrifice, resurrection, and providence reflect his deeply-held beliefs.

Tolkien's sense of wonder was closely tied to his faith. As a devout Catholic, he saw his creative process as a form of "sub-creation" – a reflection of divine creation. His faith gave him a lens through which he saw the world as a place of profound mystery, beauty, and grandeur, inspiring a sense of wonder that seeped into his writings.

Tolkien's world-building was driven by this sense of wonder. He crafted an entire universe in Middle Earth, complete with languages, races, geography, history, and mythology. Each character, plot twist, and verse of Elvish poetry was an act of exploration and discovery, an unfolding of the wonders of a world born from his imagination.

But beyond the scope of his writings, Tolkien's sense of wonder shaped his understanding of our place in the world and the divine plan. In his personal letters, Tolkien often talked about "eucatastrophe" - the sudden joyous turn in a story that reflects the grace of divine intervention. It's a concept deeply rooted in his faith and his conviction that we are all part of a divine narrative. It's this faith-based sense of wonder that encourages us to recognize our role in the divine plan and invites us to embrace it.

The tale of J.R.R. Tolkien illustrates the intimate relationship between faith and a sense of wonder. Through his faith, Tolkien saw the world and his own creative process with a sense of awe and reverence. His works encourage us to recognize the wonders in our own lives, to see the grand narrative that we are part of, and to take our unique place in it.

Tolkien's story can inspire us to look at our own lives through the lens of wonder, to see ourselves as part of a divine plan, and to follow the guidance that arises from this understanding. In so doing, we can nurture our sense of wonder, find our purpose, and, like Tolkien, use our unique gifts to inspire and uplift others.

Prophecy-

Isaiah, an ancient Hebrew prophet, is a prominent figure in the scriptures of multiple religions, including Judaism, Christianity, and Islam. He is celebrated for his compelling visions and prophecies, many of which have had enduring spiritual significance and influence over centuries.

Several of Isaiah's prophecies stand out for their far-reaching implications. Among the most notable are his predictions about the coming of a Messiah (Isaiah 9:6-7, 53), the fall and subsequent redemption of Israel (Isaiah 5:13, 10:20-22), and the future peace and prosperity of the nations under God's rule (Isaiah 2:1-4). These prophetic visions not only guided the people of his time but continue to inspire faith communities today.

However, Isaiah's experiences can also serve as an example on a more personal level. His life shows us that divine revelation, or communication from God, isn't solely reserved for prophets or significant historical figures. Rather, it is a gift available to each individual who seeks it.

In essence, personal revelation is guidance, comfort, or understanding imparted to an individual through spiritual means. It could come in response to prayer, during quiet moments of reflection, through dreams, or in the midst of life's everyday occurrences. Like Isaiah's prophecies, personal revelation often provides insight or direction at crucial moments in our lives.

Understanding Isaiah's prophecies can help us appreciate the divine guidance we receive in our lives, no matter how simple or seemingly insignificant. It teaches us that while we may not be prophets in the traditional sense, we can still be recipients of personal revelations that can guide our decisions, influence our actions, and deepen our understanding of our purpose in life.

Furthermore, Isaiah's life reminds us that receiving revelation often involves listening—quieting our minds and hearts to discern the spiritual impressions we receive. In a world full of noise and distraction, cultivating this ability to listen can be a profound spiritual practice.

By studying the life and prophecies of Isaiah, we can grow in our understanding of how divine guidance can work in our lives. As we seek this guidance and strive to follow it, we are, in our own way, walking a path similar to Isaiah's—a path toward greater wisdom, understanding, and alignment with divine will.

Healing-

Jesus Christ, known in Christian tradition as the Son of God, is a profound example of healing through faith. His ministry was marked by numerous instances of healing, providing both physical relief to those suffering and spiritual lessons to those bearing witness to His miracles.

One of the most well-known healing miracles performed by Jesus is the healing of a man born blind, as recounted in the Gospel of John (John 9:1-12). In this account, Jesus, seeing a man blind from birth, used His own saliva and some dirt to create a paste, which He then applied to the man's eyes. After washing in the pool of Siloam as instructed by Jesus, the man was able to see. This healing was not just an act of mercy; it served to affirm Jesus's divine authority and instilled faith in the onlookers.

Another remarkable healing account is found in the Gospel of Mark (Mark 5:25-34). A woman who had been suffering from a hemorrhage for twelve years, after failing to find a cure through conventional means, touched Jesus's cloak in faith, believing that this action would heal her. Jesus, sensing power had gone out from Him, turned to the crowd, and the woman confessed what she had done. He acknowledged her faith and confirmed her healing, saying, "Daughter, your faith has healed you. Go in peace and be freed from your suffering."

These healing miracles were not limited to Jesus alone. He commissioned His apostles, granting them the authority to heal in His name. In the Acts of the Apostles, we read of numerous instances where the apostles performed healing miracles, such as Peter healing a lame beggar (Acts 3:1-10) and Paul healing a crippled man in Lystra (Acts 14:8-10). These actions serve to underscore the importance of faith in bringing about miraculous healings.

What's crucial to understand is that, in these accounts, faith plays a central role. The faith of those healed, the faith of the apostles, and even the faith of the onlookers were key components in these events. And while it's true that we cannot change another's life trials or tests of faith, we can draw inspiration from these stories. We can appreciate the potential of faith in facilitating healing, in understanding, and in strengthening our compassion for those who suffer.

The stories of healing through faith remind us that we can be agents of healing in our own ways. We may not perform miraculous cures, but through our faith, love, and compassion, we can contribute to the healing of those around us—physically, emotionally, and spiritually. The essence of these healings is not just about alleviating physical suffering; it's about restoring wholeness, fostering spiritual growth, and affirming the faith that binds us all.

Miracles-

Colton Burpo's story is one that has captured global interest and inspired many. His account, as retold by his father, Todd Burpo, in the bestselling book "Heaven is for Real," presents a remarkable perspective on faith, the afterlife, and the power of personal testimony.

In 2003, Colton, then just three years old, fell critically ill due to a misdiagnosed ruptured appendix. During an emergency surgery, Colton's heart stopped, and it was during this time that he claims to have had an out-of-body experience and visited Heaven.

Colton's descriptions of Heaven were incredibly detailed, especially considering his young age. He spoke of meeting his miscarried sister, whom he had never been told about, and his great-grandfather who died 30 years before Colton was born. He described Heaven as a brilliantly bright, colorful place with a heavenly music that filled the air. According to Colton, Jesus had a horse of many colors, and everyone in Heaven had wings, except for Jesus.

Perhaps most striking was his assertion that he sat on Jesus' lap, describing Him as having "markers" (referring to the marks left by the crucifixion) and wearing a white robe with a purple sash. Colton also mentioned seeing Jesus preparing for a coming battle and emphasized that God deeply loves children.

In the years following his recovery, Colton's story spread, and "Heaven is for Real" was published in 2010. The book became a bestseller, resonating with a wide audience and later being adapted into a feature film in 2014. It spurred conversations about faith, the afterlife, and the power of spiritual experiences.

Colton's experience serves as a testament to the power of faith. It has provided comfort to many grieving the loss of loved ones, affirming beliefs in an afterlife, and serving as a source of hope. Despite skepticism from some quarters, many find solace and inspiration in Colton's vivid descriptions of Heaven and his affirmations of God's love.

Even beyond the specifics of his story, Colton Burpo's experience reminds us of the profound role faith plays in many people's lives. Faith can offer a source of hope during trials, a means of understanding profound experiences, and a way of finding comfort and peace in times of grief. Whether one fully believes Colton's account or not, the impact of his story demonstrates the power and value of faith in many people's lives.

Discernment-

Dietrich Bonhoeffer, a German pastor, theologian, and anti-Nazi dissident, provides a remarkable testament to the power of discernment rooted in faith. His life, choices, and ultimate sacrifice for his beliefs serve as an inspiring testament to his profound spiritual discernment.

Born in 1906 into an affluent intellectual family, Bonhoeffer displayed a talent for theology from a young age. Despite his family's expectation that he would follow a scientific or academic career, he discerned a different path for himself, one deeply intertwined with his Christian faith. He pursued theological studies and was ordained as a Lutheran pastor.

Bonhoeffer's faith became the guiding compass in his life, leading him to discern right from wrong even amidst the murky moral complexities of Nazi Germany. When Hitler ascended to power in 1933, Bonhoeffer was among the few Christian leaders who recognized the inherent evil of the Nazi regime. He used his talent for communication and his influence within the church community to resist the regime.

A profound moment of discernment in Bonhoeffer's life came when he chose to return to Germany from the safety of the United States in 1939. He had been offered a comfortable position at Union Theological Seminary in New York but felt a powerful call to return to his homeland, sensing that he couldn't participate in the reconstruction of Christian life in Germany after the war if he didn't share in his people's sufferings during it.

Back in Germany, Bonhoeffer's discernment led him to become an active member of the German resistance against Hitler. His faith was his compass as he grappled with difficult moral questions, such as the justification of violence for a greater cause. Despite the ethical complexity, Bonhoeffer was part of a plot to assassinate Hitler—an unthinkable act for a pastor, demonstrating the extremity of his discernment and commitment to combating evil.

Eventually, Bonhoeffer was arrested and executed in 1945, just weeks before the end of World War II. Yet, his legacy lives on. His writings, particularly "The Cost of Discipleship" and "Letters and Papers from Prison," provide deep insight into his process of discernment and his firm belief that faith should actively engage with the world.

Dietrich Bonhoeffer's life story is a powerful testament to the potential of faith-based discernment. It teaches us that discernment isn't a passive, quiet process but a dynamic, active engagement with our world—using our talents, understanding our callings, and standing firm in our beliefs even amidst great adversity. His story inspires us to embrace our faith as a guiding force, enabling us to make profound and meaningful impacts in our lives and the world around us.

Teaching-

Anne Sullivan's life story is an incredible testament to the power of faith, perseverance, and the profound impact one person can have on another's life.

Born in 1866 in Massachusetts, Sullivan faced immense adversity early in life. She lost her mother when she was just eight years old, and her father abandoned her and her younger brother not long after. Compounding these hardships, an eye infection that was not properly treated left her visually impaired. Despite these challenges, Sullivan held onto a strong belief in her capabilities and the hope for a better future, showing the first signs of a resilient faith that would become her life's cornerstone.

Sullivan was admitted to the Perkins School for the Blind at the age of 14, where she proved to be a diligent and determined student. It was here she discovered her talent for teaching and developed the faith in her ability to make a difference in someone else's life.

When she was 20, an opportunity arose that would change her life forever - teaching a seven-year-old deaf and blind girl named Helen Keller. Many had deemed the task impossible due to Keller's volatile behavior and inability to communicate, but Sullivan saw it differently. Inspired by her faith and the belief that every person, irrespective of their limitations, deserves the opportunity to learn and grow, she accepted the challenge.

Using innovative teaching techniques and an unyielding patience, Sullivan worked with Keller, teaching her to communicate through tactile sign language. She would spell out words in Keller's hand, connecting them to the objects they represented. Sullivan's faith in her student never wavered, even when progress seemed slow and the process frustrating.

Sullivan's teaching fundamentally changed Keller's life. Keller went on to become a world-renowned author, political activist, and lecturer, an unimaginable achievement without Sullivan's guidance.

However, the profound influence of Anne Sullivan extends beyond her work with Helen Keller. Her story serves as an inspiring reminder that every person, regardless of their life circumstances, holds the potential to change the world in their unique way. We are all teachers in our own right, imparting knowledge, values, and inspiration to those we interact with in our daily lives.

It's important to remember that the impact we make may not always be visible to us. We may not have the chance to see the seeds of wisdom we plant in others grow and flourish. However, just like Anne Sullivan, we should maintain our faith in the difference we can make and fulfill our unique callings with dedication and passion. By doing so, we can create ripples of change that extend far beyond our immediate perception, contributing to a better, more understanding world.

Encouragement-

Rosa Parks, a name widely recognized as a symbol of courage, dignity, and determination, was a woman whose steadfast faith became a cornerstone of the American Civil Rights Movement. Her story is a powerful testament to how an individual's faith and courage can inspire and encourage change, even in the face of significant adversity.

Born in 1913 in Tuskegee, Alabama, Rosa Louise McCauley Parks was brought up in an era marked by rampant racial segregation and discrimination. Her grandparents, former slaves, and her mother, a teacher, instilled in her a strong sense of dignity and a deep Christian faith. This upbringing would later become the driving force behind her unwavering resolve to stand against injustice.

The pivotal moment that placed Parks in the annals of history occurred on December 1, 1955, in Montgomery, Alabama. After a long day's work as a seamstress, Parks boarded a city bus to return home. She found a seat in the 'colored section', toward the middle of the bus. As the bus filled up, a white man boarded, and when no seats were available in the 'white section', the bus driver ordered Parks and three other black passengers to give up their seats.

In an act of quiet but firm defiance, Parks refused to surrender her seat. Her resistance wasn't a product of physical exhaustion, as some might assume, but a profound spiritual and moral exhaustion. She later said, "The only tired I was, was tired of giving in."

Parks was arrested for her refusal to obey the segregation laws of the time. Her arrest became a catalyst for the Montgomery Bus Boycott, a massive protest that lasted 381 days, demonstrating the power of collective action against racial segregation.

Parks' act of defiance and her subsequent arrest wasn't a spontaneous decision but a reflection of her strong faith and belief in equality. As a long-standing member of the National Association for the Advancement of Colored People (NAACP), she had been an active part of the struggle for racial equality. Her faith not only instilled in her the courage to stand up against injustice, but it also encouraged others to take similar actions.

Rosa Parks' story serves as a reminder that faith can imbue us with the courage to stand against injustice and the strength to endure in the face of adversity. Her refusal to yield her seat was not just an act of defiance against racial segregation; it was a proclamation of faith in the fundamental rights and freedoms of all individuals. Her story encourages us to stand firm in our convictions, demonstrating that even seemingly small acts of courage can ignite substantial change.

We may not find ourselves in situations as dire as Rosa Parks', but we each face our own trials and tribulations. And it's during these times that our faith can inspire us to act, to stand firm, and to encourage others to do the same. Whether it's supporting a friend during a tough time, standing up for what's right, or spreading kindness in a world that sometimes seems void of it, every act of faith and encouragement contributes to the betterment of our collective human experience.

Mercy-

Oskar Schindler was a German industrialist and member of the Nazi Party who is best known for his remarkable act of mercy during the Holocaust, saving the lives of over 1,100 Jews by employing them in his factories. His story was popularized by Thomas Keneally's 1982 novel "Schindler's Ark," and Steven Spielberg's 1993 film "Schindler's List."

Schindler initially saw his workers as a means to profit, as using Jewish labor was cheaper than using non-Jewish labor. But over time, through the horrors he witnessed, Schindler's perspective dramatically shifted. He started to see the intrinsic human value of his Jewish workers and was moved by a sense of compassion and mercy that prompted him to risk his own life to save theirs.

Though he was not openly religious, some argue that Schindler exhibited a faith in humanity and its capacity for goodness, which fueled his actions. He demonstrated a belief in the sanctity of human life, the very core of many religious beliefs. He expended his entire fortune to bribe Nazi officials to keep his workers safe, ultimately saving them from the brutalities of the Holocaust.

The impact of Schindler's actions continues to reverberate today, with the descendants of "Schindler's Jews" numbering in the thousands. His life stands as a testament to the power of mercy, even in the face of profound evil, and his story remains a beacon of hope and humanity amidst the darkness of one of history's most tragic periods. His unwavering courage and dedication to preserve life, against all odds, has continued to inspire generations, highlighting the indomitable power of mercy and compassion.

Desmond Tutu, a South African Anglican bishop and social rights activist, is renowned globally for his role in ending apartheid and promoting racial reconciliation in South Africa. His deep faith and strong belief in the Christian values of love, forgiveness, and mercy guided his actions throughout this tumultuous period in South African history.

Tutu staunchly opposed apartheid, the institutionalized racial segregation enforced by the National Party government of South Africa. His spiritual convictions led him to advocate for nonviolent resistance and civil disobedience against unjust laws, drawing inspiration from figures like Mahatma Gandhi and Martin Luther King Jr. Tutu's commitment to equality and justice, grounded in his faith, earned him the Nobel Peace Prize in 1984.

Following the end of apartheid, Tutu was appointed by Nelson Mandela to chair the Truth and Reconciliation Commission (TRC) in 1995. The TRC was established to uncover the atrocities committed during apartheid and to promote healing and reconciliation. Instead of seeking punishment, the TRC granted amnesty to those who fully disclosed their politically motivated crimes.

This was an act of mercy on a national scale, based on Tutu's belief in "Ubuntu" - an African philosophy suggesting that we affirm our own humanity by recognizing the humanity in others. By facilitating a process of truth-telling and forgiveness, Tutu hoped to mend the deep societal fractures caused by decades of racial oppression.

Desmond Tutu's life and work demonstrate how mercy, when coupled with a commitment to justice and reconciliation, can be a powerful force for societal healing. His legacy continues to inspire peace and reconciliation efforts around the world, and serves as a testament to the transformative power of mercy in overcoming systemic injustice.

Abraham Lincoln, the 16th President of the United States, is often cited as a historic example of leadership marked by mercy. His commitment to preserving the Union during the Civil War, while simultaneously striving to end the institution of slavery, required both a steadfast commitment to principles and a considerable capacity for mercy.

One of Lincoln's most notable acts of mercy came with the Emancipation Proclamation in 1862, which declared enslaved people in Confederate-held territories free, altering the course of the Civil War and the nation's history. This was not only a strategic move in the war effort but also a profound act of mercy toward those who had been enslaved.

In his second inaugural address in 1865, amidst the concluding days of the Civil War, Lincoln's emphasis was not on victory, but on healing. His call for "malice toward none" and "charity for all" was a call for mercy, embodying a vision of reconciliation and unity. It was a remarkable expression of mercy toward the South, where many held Lincoln responsible for the devastation the war had wrought.

Lincoln's approach toward the defeated South after the Civil War is seen as embodying mercy. His primary concern was to heal the nation and reintegrate the Southern states into the Union, rather than punishing them for the rebellion. This approach, known as the "Ten Percent Plan," aimed at swift reconciliation with minimal retribution.

The faith that guided Lincoln was a complex and deeply personal one. He was not formally affiliated with any church, but his speeches and writings reflect a deep belief in God's providence and the moral duty of individuals and nations. He once said, "I have been driven many times upon my knees by the overwhelming conviction that I had nowhere else to go. My own wisdom and that of all about me seemed insufficient for that day."

The legacy of Lincoln's mercy endures in the continued pursuit of a more just and equitable America. His leadership during one of the nation's most fraught periods serves as a testament to the power of mercy and compassion in leading a divided nation toward reconciliation.

Mahatma Gandhi, often referred to as the "Father of the Nation" in India, is globally recognized as a symbol of nonviolent resistance and mercy. His philosophy and lifestyle were deeply rooted in the concept of 'Ahimsa,' which translates to 'non-violence,' and extended to showing compassion and mercy toward all living beings.

Gandhi was an ardent believer in truth and advocated for peaceful means to accomplish political and social goals. He led India's struggle for independence from British rule using nonviolent civil disobedience, inspiring movements for civil rights and freedom worldwide.

One of the defining moments of Gandhi's show of mercy was his response to the 1919 Jallianwala Bagh massacre. In response to the violent act by British forces, instead of promoting revenge, he intensified his nonviolent resistance, rallying the nation behind peaceful protests.

His philosophy of mercy and forgiveness is reflected in his reaction to the violent outbreaks during the partition of India in 1947. Despite the massive communal violence between Hindus and Muslims, Gandhi preached unity, forgiveness, and reconciliation, even going on a fast unto death to protest against the violence.

Gandhi's faith was a blend of Hinduism, Jainism, Christianity, and other religious influences, emphasizing truth, non-violence, and compassion toward all beings. His famous quote, "an eye for an eye only ends up making the whole world blind," encapsulates his belief in mercy over revenge.

Gandhi's legacy continues to have a global impact, inspiring countless movements for civil rights, freedom, and justice. His life and teachings have shown that mercy and non-violence can indeed bring about significant social and political change, demonstrating the potential of peaceful means in resolving conflicts.

Acts of mercy don't have to be grand or highly visible to make a significant difference. Small gestures of kindness and compassion can have a profound impact on the lives of others and can even create a ripple effect of goodwill. One such story that comes to mind is a real-life incident involving a woman named Laura Schroff.

In 1986, Laura, an advertising executive, was walking down a street in Manhattan when she was approached by an 11-year-old boy named Maurice. He asked her for spare change because he was hungry. Rather than simply giving him money and moving on, Laura decided to do something more. She took Maurice to a McDonald's nearby and they shared a meal together.

What was initially meant to be a one-time act of mercy turned into a weekly tradition. Every Monday for the next four years, Laura and Maurice would meet for dinner. During these meals, she not only fed him but also got to know him, and ultimately became a positive, stable force in his tumultuous life.

Laura didn't have to do something monumental to make a difference in Maurice's life. Her simple act of shared meals and conversations served as an anchor for a young boy navigating a difficult childhood. This act of mercy didn't just feed Maurice's hunger for food, it also addressed his hunger for kindness, stability, and human connection.

This story was eventually chronicled in the book "An Invisible Thread," illustrating how powerful such small acts of mercy can be. The impact on Maurice's life was immense. In a later interview, he said, "If Laura never approached me or accepted me into her life, I would probably be dead."

This story is a powerful reminder that the most profound acts of mercy often happen in the small, everyday moments of life. It's an invitation for all of us to embody mercy in our own lives. You never know how a small act of kindness can change someone's life, or even your own. So let's approach the world with more understanding, more kindness, and more mercy. Every small act of mercy brings us one step closer to a more compassionate and empathetic world.

As we navigate through these rich narratives, we witness the marvelous diversity in the expression of faith. We begin to understand that faith is not a rigid, one-dimensional concept, but a vibrant mosaic of diverse beliefs and experiences.

Moreover, this diversity is not confined to our local community but extends across the globe, encompassing different cultures, traditions, and religions. Each faith tradition contributes a unique note to this divine symphony, adding richness and depth to our understanding.

Just as there have been remarkable individuals throughout history who have shown us the transformative power of faith, each one of us has the potential to touch the divine in our unique ways. In our personal faith journey, it's vital to remember that faith isn't a fixed point, but an ongoing voyage of discovery and growth.

Like a seed that transforms into a magnificent tree, faith too begins as a mere spark, a question, or a moment of awe, growing over time, nurtured by experience, understanding, and introspection. This process of growth and evolution forms the very essence of faith.

As we near the end of this chapter, I hope you feel inspired to delve into your spiritual gifts, engaging with your faith in ways that resonate with your spiritual journey, and contributing your unique note to this symphony of faith. Each of you possesses a unique note that adds depth and richness to this grand mural of faith.

Faith is a journey toward understanding, acceptance, and unity, embracing the diversity of human experiences and underscoring our shared spiritual aspirations. As you embark on your faith journey, remember, we are all part of this grand narrative, each a torchbearer of our unique spiritual gifts, collectively adding to the legacy of faith.

Your journey, your questions, your discoveries, and your expressions of faith are all invaluable threads in the intricate web of our shared faith heritage. You are a vital part of this legacy.

So, step forward and let your faith illuminate your path and inspire others on their journey toward the divine. Your spiritual gifts are a beacon of hope, shedding light on your path and inspiring others on their quest for the divine. You are a vital participant in this shared legacy. Embrace your unique gifts and contribute to the radiant light of faith.

CHAPTER THIRTY ONE

A Guiding Light: Faith as a Lighthouse in the Stormy Seas of Morality and Ethics

A lighthouse amidst a stormy sea, a compass pointing true north, a shepherd guiding its flock - these are all metaphors that encapsulate the role of faith as a guiding principle in our lives. Beyond a mere belief in the divine or adherence to religious scriptures, faith shapes our moral and ethical compass, illuminating the intricate labyrinth of human interaction and decision-making. It burns brightly within us, providing solace and guidance in times of uncertainty, its beacon shedding light on the right path in the sometimes-foggy journey of life.

Let us ponder the real-life saga of Malala Yousafzai, a young Pakistani girl who dared to defy the oppressive regime of the Taliban for her fundamental right to education. Animated by her indomitable faith, she braved death threats and bodily harm, tenaciously advocating for girls' education. It was her faith that became her guiding star in the enveloping darkness, not a tether that held her back but a compass guiding her forward. It imbued her with a sense of justice and courage, compelling her to stand up against systemic oppression. Her resilience and commitment in the face of adversity offer a compelling testimony to the ways in which faith can inform and inspire our moral and ethical decisions.

To further explore this principle, let us journey into a fictional universe. Picture Jonah, a successful executive in a towering corporation located in a sprawling metropolis. Despite being surrounded by wealth, status, and power, Jonah remains tethered to his deeply ingrained faith. It is this faith that shapes his interactions, compelling him to extend kindness and respect to everyone, irrespective of their position in the corporate hierarchy. His faith reminds him of the inherent dignity of every individual and drives him to maintain ethical and sustainable business practices, mirroring the teachings of his faith about stewardship and responsibility.

A corporate decision tests Jonah's moral fiber: his company plans to launch a lucrative development project that threatens to uproot a marginalized community. The project promises hefty profits but at the steep cost of displacing people from their homes. Torn between personal gain and ethical responsibility, Jonah grapples with his decision.

In this ethical quagmire, Jonah seeks refuge in his faith. He immerses himself in prayer, revisits the tenets of his religion, and solicits advice from his spiritual mentors. This introspective journey reignites the fundamental principles of his faith—compassion, justice, and respect for the dignity of all individuals.

Armed with moral clarity, Jonah chooses the path less trodden. He raises his voice against the project, aligning himself with the rights of the marginalized community. This decision invites substantial backlash, and he risks losing his executive position. But, anchored by his faith and its ethical guidance, he remains resolute. He uses his influence to propose an alternative, socially responsible project, showcasing the harmonious coexistence of faith, morality, and success.

Jonah's narrative casts a spotlight on how faith can serve as a lighthouse in the stormy seas of ethical dilemmas. It underlines that faith, far from promoting division, can be a catalyst for unity, acceptance, and compassion. It can embolden us to champion justice, lend our voices to the voiceless, and strive for a world rich in compassion and equity.

Faith, in its purest form, is an all-embracing force. It encourages us to look beyond our differences, acknowledging the divine spark within every individual. It emphasizes our shared existence in this grand celestial landscape, reminding us of our collective values of love, respect, and dignity.

Navigating the tumultuous seas of life, faith serves as our spiritual anchor. It impels us to embody compassion, uphold justice, and foster an inclusive world where each individual, regardless of their origins, is cherished and respected.

May this serve as a touchstone in your journey of faith, a lighthouse that illuminates your path. Let it inspire your actions, guide your decisions, and remind you of the transformative power of faith in molding a more empathetic, compassionate, and equitable world.

CHAPTER THIRTY TWO

Interpreting the Divine: Faith in a Higher Power

Faith is a celestial river, flowing unseen through the vast universe of our experiences. It permeates various dimensions of our lives—our relationships, our communities, our trust in leaders and institutions. But at the heart of this faith cosmos often lies a belief in a higher power. This belief, transcending tangible realities, serves as a spiritual compass, imbuing our life with a profound sense of purpose.

Let's explore this concept through the faith journey of Maya, a successful architect nestled in the urban jungle of a bustling city. Maya, a practical thinker, anchored her life firmly in the material world. She placed her faith in the solidity of concrete structures and steel frameworks, finding beauty and certainty in the tangible world she shaped and navigated.

Her universe comprised of blueprints and building plans, her faith lay in the structures she meticulously crafted. This perspective, tethered to the physical, resonated with her. However, an unforeseen encounter with nature catalyzed a transformative shift in her understanding of the world.

One fateful day, a storm rolled in unexpectedly while Maya was out in the city. She took shelter in a nearby park, where amidst the fury of the tempest, her gaze fell on an enormous, ancient oak tree. This grand entity stood firm and unscathed, its branches reaching towards the tumultuous skies as if in prayer, its roots delving deep into the nurturing earth.

In that moment, the oak tree became a living testament to a force greater than the visible world. Its roots mirrored the unseen foundations of Maya's architectural marvels; its upward growth reflected her aspirations. She felt a parallel between the oak tree and her own life—both were parts of a grander ecosystem, drawing sustenance and strength from sources unseen and often unacknowledged.

This transformative encounter germinated a seed of faith within Maya. She began to embrace the idea of a force greater than herself—a divine, creative power steering the cosmos. This newfound faith did not diminish her accomplishments or self-reliance; instead, it enriched them with a deeper meaning and purpose.

Now, Maya's architectural endeavors transformed. Her work transcended from merely creating buildings to becoming an active participant in the grand design she felt intimately connected to. Every blueprint she drafted, every building she erected, became an act of co-creation with the divine force she had begun to acknowledge.

Albert Einstein once remarked, "Everyone who is seriously involved in the pursuit of science becomes convinced that a spirit is manifest in the laws of the universe—a spirit vastly superior to that of man." Maya's journey mirrors this sentiment. Faith in a higher power isn't about surrendering control or denying one's capabilities. It's about recognizing our place within the grand scheme of things, acknowledging that we are threads in a cosmic matrix whose expanse stretches far beyond our comprehension.

Each faith journey is deeply personal, as unique as the individual undertaking it. Your higher power may assume the form of God, the Universe, the Laws of Nature, or Love itself. The nature of this higher power, while personal, often provides a profound sense of direction, a spiritual rudder guiding us through the turbulent seas of life.

As we traverse the vast landscape of faith, let's celebrate the diversity in our beliefs. Let's approach differing perspectives not with judgment but with curiosity and respect. Each path to faith is as unique as the individual journeying on it, and in this shared exploration, we can find common ground—a collective sense of purpose and unity.

Remember, faith is not a final destination but an ongoing journey—an open-ended exploration of the mysterious, a call to engage with life's profound enigmas. It's about seeking connection—with ourselves, with others, and with the divine. It's about finding purpose in the grand spectacle of existence and resonating with the cosmic rhythm of life.

In the end, faith in a higher power serves as a guiding star, casting its luminous glow on our path through life. It's a beacon of hope in times of despair, a compass guiding us through tumultuous seas, and ultimately, a bridge connecting our finite human experiences with the infinite cosmic dance. This profound connection fosters a sense of belonging, unity, and an understanding of our significant yet humble role in the greater narrative of life.

CHAPTER THIRTY THREE

The Intimate Act of Faith: Personal Prayers, Genuine Devotion, and The Art of Daily Practice

On the broad canvas of faith, we encounter a diverse array of rituals, prayers, and acts of devotion, each serving as a unique bridge connecting us with the divine. However, true faith, the kind that delves into the deepest reaches of our souls, isn't solely encapsulated within these traditional routines. Instead, it flourishes in the most intimate and authentic spaces of our lives – in the quiet whispers of heartfelt prayer, in the selfless gestures that spring from compassion, and in our personal communion with the divine.

Reflect on the teachings of Jesus, who imparted a profound understanding of prayer in the Book of Matthew (6:6): "But when you pray, go into your room, close the door and pray to your Father, who is unseen. Then your Father, who sees what is done in secret, will reward you." Jesus emphasized that prayer is not a performance for an audience but a private, personal communion with God. This principle of solitary prayer serves as a potent reminder that faith requires no stage; it finds a home in the quiet corners of our hearts, offering a steady anchor in life's tumultuous seas.

Let's observe Maya, a spiritual seeker embarking on a quest for inner peace and guidance. Rather than reciting rote prayers, Maya engages in a heartfelt dialogue with her Creator—an exchange steeped in sincerity, love, and trust. In this personalized communication, she discovers faith as a living, breathing entity that stems not from a sense of duty, but from a genuine longing for a deeper connection.

In parallel, we can learn from David, a man deeply rooted in religious practice. Over time, he realizes that the essence of devotion extends beyond mere external rituals. True devotion resides in the sincerity and intent that fuels the action, rather than the action itself. Enlightened by this insight, David redirects his faith toward acts of service, compassion, and kindness, recognizing the divine within himself and others. His faith becomes a beacon guiding him to honor the sacred in all life forms, fostering a spirit of unity, goodwill, and love.

Faith is not confined to prayer mats, pews, or meditation cushions; it permeates our day-to-day existence. Take Hope, a school teacher who embodies this truth. Guided by her faith, she views her profession not just as a job but as a divine calling to nurture young minds and hearts. Through her dedication and love, she enlightens and inspires, regarding her abilities as divine gifts to be used for the upliftment of others. Hope's actions reflect faith in action, a testament to faith's power as a catalyst for positive societal transformation.

Indeed, rituals, prayers, and acts of devotion provide a structure to express our beliefs. But the heart of faith lies not in these practices but in the openness of our hearts to the divine. It blossoms from an intimate relationship with our Creator, a delicate dance of learning, growth, and deep connection.

As we engage in personal dialogues with the divine, perform acts of genuine devotion, and translate our faith into acts of service and kindness, we truly embody the essence of living faith. The practice of faith, in this sense, becomes a journey of continual growth and compassion, propelling us towards a life imbued with a deeper sense of purpose.

Let these narratives inspire you to nurture a living faith—one that resides in the deepest recesses of your heart and permeates every aspect of your existence. Embrace this faith through personal dialogue with the divine, genuine acts of devotion, and the selfless use of your divine gifts. In doing so, you not only solidify your relationship with your Creator but also transform your life into a testament of faith's transformative power, finding solace, fortitude, and renewed purpose at every step of your journey.

CHAPTER THIRTY FOUR

The Legacy of Faith: Passing on the Torch of Belief

In the multilayered framework of human existence, we find compelling narratives that further illuminate this concept. Let's review the story of James, a man who was immersed in scientific pursuits and held a deeply rational outlook on life. James often found it challenging to accept anything that couldn't be verified by empirical evidence, including the concept of faith. He struggled to understand how individuals could place their trust in an unseen entity and how they could derive solace from this inexplicable connection.

However, a life-altering event disrupted his rigid worldview. Following a severe car accident, James found himself in a long and painful period of recovery. He felt lonely and desolate, cut off from his previous life, his identity as a vibrant, independent individual disintegrated. One day, a hospital volunteer named Mary visited him. Mary was a woman of profound faith, and she shared her perspective on life, suffering, and the role of faith in navigating the challenging terrains of human existence.

Initially, James dismissed her ideas as wishful thinking. However, as his suffering persisted, he found himself revisiting Mary's words, contemplating the idea of faith. His rational mind initially resisted, seeking empirical evidence. Yet, in the depths of his despair, he found his heart opening up to the possibility of faith.

James started exploring faith, not as a scientific concept, but as a deeply personal experience. He learned to pray, not by rote, but as an authentic expression of his feelings and desires. James discovered faith not as a rational concept but as a relationship, a dialogue with a higher power that offered him solace, strength, and purpose.

This experience transformed James. His worldview expanded to include both the empirical and the experiential, the rational and the spiritual. He realized that his previous focus on the scientific and rational had prevented him from perceiving the spiritual dimensions of existence. He learned that faith, like color in a picture, could be overlooked if one's attention was directed elsewhere.

James' story serves as a powerful testament to the transformative power of faith and the importance of an open heart and mind. His journey reflects the profound connection between the heart and the mind and the importance of engaging both in the realm of faith. His story illustrates how faith is not merely an alien concept to be analyzed and understood. It is an intimate relationship to be experienced, a dormant spark within us waiting to be kindled into a vibrant flame.

As we continue our shared journey into the realm of faith, let's remember the lesson from James' story: Faith is not just a solitary endeavor but a shared legacy. It is an illuminating torch that we are entrusted to carry and pass on, casting a radiant glow on our paths and those around us. As we navigate our path with an open heart and mind, we allow ourselves to perceive the full spectrum of faith's beauty, mystery, and profound depth, enriching our journey and the journeys of those around us.

CHAPTER THIRTY FIVE

One Destination, Many Paths: Embracing the Unity of Faith

Within the intricate weave of our collective experience, there exists a remarkable unity that transcends the boundaries of faith. As we embark on this exploration of diverse spiritual paths, let us embrace the interconnectedness that binds us together and illuminates our shared destination.

Examine the captivating stories of Maya, Abraham, Amina, and Jack, individuals from different corners of the world whose faith journeys exemplify the beauty of our collective spiritual heritage. Their paths, though diverse in practice and belief, ultimately converge toward the same transcendent truth, beckoning us to discover the harmony that lies beneath the surface.

Maya, a young girl born into a Buddhist family in Thailand, was enveloped in the teachings of the Buddha. Her journey revolved around the understanding of Dukkha (suffering), Anicca (impermanence), and Anatta (non-self). Guided by compassion and mindfulness, Maya sought to alleviate suffering and find a profound peace, believing it to be the very nature of our divine source. Though her path was steeped in the rituals and traditions of Buddhism, at its core was a universal longing shared by all humanity—a desire to transcend suffering and connect with something greater than ourselves.

In the bustling city of New York, Abraham, a deeply committed Jewish man, found solace in his faith. The teachings of the Torah illuminated his path, emphasizing the importance of performing mitzvot and instilling an enduring hope in the coming of the Messiah. Every Sabbath, as he recited prayers steeped in tradition, Abraham experienced a divine presence that felt both ancient and immediate. His journey, unique to the Jewish faith, echoed Maya's pursuit of peace and divine connection, revealing the underlying unity of their shared spiritual journey.

Meanwhile, in the heart of Nigeria, Amina, a young Muslim woman, discovered her faith intertwined with the five pillars of Islam. Her path was marked by the beauty of daily prayers, the reverence of fasting during Ramadan, the intention to embark on the Hajj pilgrimage, and the commitment to offering Zakat. Amina's journey, distinctly Islamic in its expression, echoed the universal theme present in Maya's and Abraham's experiences—a deep longing for connection with the divine source and a commitment to live in alignment with its perceived will.

Amidst this exploration, let us not forget Jack, an ordinary college student from Sydney, Australia. Unbeknownst to him, he too is on a path of faith. In his acts of kindness, moments of wonder at the universe, and connections forged with others, Jack unknowingly embodies the divine presence in the world. His life, like every life, is touched by the divine, carrying within it the potential for spiritual growth and a deepening understanding of our shared humanity.

From Maya's Buddhist meditation in Thailand, through Abraham's Jewish prayers in New York, Amina's

Islamic practices in Nigeria, to Jack's acts of kindness in Australia, the divine subtly beckons. In ways we may or may not realize, through ancient traditions and new expressions of faith, our lives are interwoven with the divine. Our paths may diverge, taking on unique hues and melodies, yet each step we take, each act of kindness, and each moment of reverence and wonder is a testament to our shared spiritual journey.

These stories, drawn from different corners of the world, reveal the remarkable unity inherent in our diverse faith traditions. They serve as a testament to the power of spirituality to transcend barriers and create bridges of understanding. Whether we find ourselves in a Buddhist temple in Thailand, a synagogue in New York, a mosque in Nigeria, or simply walking the streets of our hometown, we are all walking paths that, while unique, are connected by a shared destination.

Let us cherish the universal thread weaving through each story—the call to connect with something greater than ourselves, a divine source that fuels our desire to seek meaning, cultivate compassion, and strive for inner peace. In celebrating our shared destination, we embrace the profound realization that, despite our varied paths, one day, all of humanity will find unity in this sacred truth.

May this belief, rooted in the interconnectedness of faith, bring solace and anticipation to your heart as we embark on this remarkable journey together.

CHAPTER THIRTY SIX

The Unyielding Flame: A Journey of Faith and Purpose

If one believes in a singular, benevolent Creator, a God who wishes for the prosperity of all His children, it's compelling to imagine His grand plan unfolding much like this:

Before we drew our first breath in the realm of mortality, we might have resided in a pre-existing spirit world, a world radiant with love, light, and harmony. Here, we could recognize ourselves as the divine progeny of our Creator, a being of infinite wisdom, compassion, and incomprehensible love.

We may have understood that our journey would extend beyond this mortal life, carrying us toward a divine destiny that was far beyond our human imagination. We could see our earthly existence as a stepping stone—an arena for faith and growth—designed to help us realize this divine destiny.

In this pre-mortal realm, we might have been granted a precious gift, the gift of agency. We could have understood that our choices had the power to shape our souls and that true faith could only be cultivated through the exercise of this free will. While we could acknowledge our choices might lead to pain and suffering, we may have also known that the divine light within us would serve as a compass, guiding us through our trials.

The spirits we were could have pledged to uplift one another throughout our mortal journey. We may have known that the bonds of unity and love forged in the pre-existence would transcend mortality and persist through eternity. And so, filled with hope, we descended from this realm of light and love into the world of mortality.

Our mortal world, while bound by natural laws and not subject to divine intervention that could break these laws, could have been intricately designed to help us discern truth, navigate adversity, and discover our inner strength.

Every person you see might have embarked on this sacred journey, each with their unique path etched in the grand fresco of life. They would encounter diverse circumstances, face individual trials, and grapple with the complexities of their existence. But within their hearts, a vestige of celestial memory could have lingered, fueling their yearning to reconnect with their divine heritage.

Throughout this mortal odyssey, they could discover the transformative power of faith, hope, and love. The acts of charity and selflessness they performed could bear testimony to the truth that pure love—the love of a parent for their child—resided at the heart of their heavenly parents.

Some may lose their way amidst the shadows of doubt and despair. Yet, their spiritual brothers and sisters might stand firm, embracing the fallen and guiding them back toward the path of righteousness. They could understand that each soul's destiny was not defined by its stumbles, but by the unwavering commitment to rise again, learn, and grow.

Even the most perplexing moments, the deepest pains, and the greatest joys could serve a purpose. They might realize that every twist and turn of their journey was part of their soul's development, moulding them into beings capable of comprehending the unfathomable beauty that awaited beyond the veil of mortality.

So, dear reader, you too could be a cherished spirit on a path of faith, growth, and divine purpose. Let the story of your pre-mortal existence, should it be true, ignite a spark of curiosity within you, drawing you closer to the light of truth.

Remember that you are cradled in the arms of your loving heavenly parents, who watch over you with tender care. As you journey through life, make wise choices, for they shape your soul and align you with the divine plan.

Take solace in the knowledge that while challenges and uncertainties may arise, your inner light of wisdom remains ever-present. Seek that light, follow your heart, and extend a helping hand to those around you. For in the shared commitment to uplift and support one another, lies the essence of your divine nature.

And as you navigate through the ebb and flow of mortal existence, hold onto the belief that one day, everything will make sense. The paths you tread, the lessons you learned, and the love you shared will come together in a symphony of understanding.

May this story of faith, compassion, and eternal progression fill your heart and inspire you to embark on your own journey of discovery. Embrace the divine within you, for you are destined for remarkable greatness. And remember that you are a cherished child of a loving Creator. Let these words guide you toward a life of purpose, joy, and eternal fulfillment.

The Infinite Journey: Continuing the Quest for Deeper Faith

'm deeply grateful that you've journeyed with me through these pages, exploring the profound depths of faith and its transformative potential. It's been a privilege to share with you, and my humble hope is that these words have sparked an interest, kindled a curiosity, and perhaps even ignited a desire to delve deeper into the richness of faith. In the wisdom of Christ, as He beckons us to humble ourselves like children, we find an invigorating challenge for the road ahead.

Indeed, the stories and insights shared here are not merely words on a page. They're invitations – invitations to explore, to question, to seek, and to embrace an attitude of childlike wonder. Yet, they also call for maturity, learned through the trials and triumphs of life. In the spirit of Christ's teachings, can we harmonize these seemingly contrasting facets? Yes, indeed, we can - and we must.

Just like the pure heart of a child, unencumbered by the fetters of impossibility, we too should approach life with open hearts and boundless dreams. This, however, does not mean abandoning our maturity, our wisdom. On the contrary, we must hold it close, merging it with our newfound openness. As Christ suggested, let us bring the attitude of a child to the vast expanse of our experience.

This amalgamation – of openness and wisdom, of childish audacity and mature understanding – that's where we find our strength. It empowers us to face the roadblocks of fear, the shackles of complacency, to tread into the world where success is within our reach. It allows us to magnify our talents, to reach new heights, to become all that we've ever dreamed of. Thus, let this be your challenge – to integrate this attitude into your life, carrying all you've learned along the path of faith.

Remember, faith is not a destination, but a journey, an exciting journey. Each question, each doubt, each moment of wonder propels you towards deeper understanding and connection. As you embark on this path, bring with you the lessons learned, the wisdom acquired, but also the unabashed openness of a child, unafraid to dream.

Thank you for sharing this journey with me. May these words serve as seeds, sown in the fertile ground of your curiosity. May they grow into a vibrant, thriving faith, casting light on your path, and inspiring others to embark on their journeys.

Here's to a journey of faith, hope, and discovery. Here's to the transformative power of belief, and the countless ways it can shape and enrich our lives. Let this book not be the end, but the beginning of an exciting, life-changing journey for you. May it stir your heart, challenge your perceptions, and inspire you to strive towards the realization of your dreams. This is the spirit of faith, the spirit of hope, the spirit of a journey unending.

As I close this book, I can't help but envision the cover - a captivating scene that mirrors the essence of our faith journey. Picture a serene lake stretching out before you, its tranquil waters reflecting the hues of the beauty that surrounds us. A woman sits on a secure dock, looking towards the horizon. Though her face is turned away, there is a radiant glow surrounding her, hinting at the boundless hope that fills her heart. She sees clearly what lies ahead, a glorious and promising future.

This image encapsulates the spirit of our faith, a journey of hope and discovery, much like the one we've embarked upon together through these pages. As we gaze at this cover, let it remind us of the hope that faith instills in us, both individually and collectively. Hope is a powerful force, capable of lighting up even the darkest corners of our lives.

Throughout this book, we've explored the profound significance of faith in various aspects of our existence - as individuals, as families, as communities, and as a society. We've witnessed how faith can be expressed in countless ways, inspiring people to give of themselves selflessly and enriching their own lives in the process.

We've delved into the many facets of faith, learning that it's not merely an abstract concept but a dynamic force that grows and evolves with us. It's an ever-unfolding journey, not a fixed destination. Each challenge we encounter, each trial we face, becomes a stepping stone toward greater understanding and a stronger foundation for our faith.

Looking back, it's easy to see how faith has shaped our lives and led us to where we are today. But looking forward and living in the present takes trust and courage. It requires us to embrace uncertainty and walk boldly into the unknown, holding onto the light of hope that guides us through the shadows.

And so, as we stand in the present and peer into the future, let us do so with unwavering faith. Despite the trials that surround us, let us keep our eyes fixed on the bright light ahead. With the spirit of hope in our hearts, we shall overcome these challenges and shape a better future for ourselves and the generations to come.

Faith is not a solitary endeavor; it's a collective journey that binds us together. As we face the uncertain path ahead, let us remember that we are not alone. Together, we can support and uplift one another, infusing our souls with the light of hope and igniting a flame that will illuminate the way forward.

As we part ways, may the seeds of faith sown in your heart through these words flourish and grow into a thriving belief that sustains you through all of life's twists and turns. Let the transformative power of faith shape your thoughts, actions, and aspirations, allowing you to reach new heights and fulfill the dreams that reside within you.

This book may be drawing to a close, but the journey of faith is unending. Let it be the beginning of a new chapter in your life - a chapter filled with hope, gratitude, and a relentless pursuit of deeper faith. Together, we can reshape our society, infusing it with the guiding light of faith, and steering it towards a brighter and more compassionate future.

In the spirit of this infinite journey, I extend my deepest gratitude to you, dear reader, for accompanying me on this exploration. Let us carry the flame of hope and faith in our hearts and inspire others to join us on this transformative path.

Here's to the unending journey of faith, hope, and discovery. May it swell within us and shine brightly for all to see. And together, with unwavering certainty, let us forge ahead into a future filled with boundless hope and endless possibilities.

www.ingramcontent.com/pod-product-compliance
Lightning Source LLC
Chambersburg PA
CBHW032009050726
47590CB00006B/2108